50 WALKS
ON THE
ESSEX COAST

PETER CATON

Matador
9 Priory Business Park,
Wistow Road, Kibworth Beauchamp,
Leicestershire. LE8 0RX
Tel: 0116 279 2299
Email: books@troubador.co.uk
Web: www.troubador.co.uk/matador
Twitter: @matadorbooks

ISBN 978 1785892 578

British Library Cataloguing in Publication Data.
A catalogue record for this book is available from the British Library.

Printed and bound in Czech Republic by PB Print
Typeset in 11pt Gill Sans by Troubador Publishing Ltd, Leicester, UK

Matador is an imprint of Troubador Publishing Ltd

Peter Caton was born in 1960 and has always lived in Upminster, Essex. He is married with two children. After training as a polymer chemist, he set up his own business testing and manufacturing adhesives. He has a keen interest in walking, the countryside and conservation and is a member of many environmental organisations. His other interests include travelling and football (he is a West Ham season ticket holder) and he is a member of Upminster Methodist Church.

With thanks to all my friends who helped check the walks, particularly Brian Webb and to David Lothian, my wife Debbie and my parents for assistance with proof reading.

The Walks

Introduction

With the longest coastline of any English county, the creeks, estuaries and sea walls of Essex provide ample opportunity for varied walking. Some, like the promenades around Southend or Clacton, is well known, but most is quiet and enjoyed by just a few walkers and birdwatchers. Parts of the Essex coast are some of the remotest in England but with no hills, walking is easy.

I have described walks including the entire publicly accessible Essex coast to the first fixed crossing point (which generally is around the tidal limit), so should you wish to walk it from end to end the book can be used as a guide. Most readers will however be looking for shorter, ideally circular walks, so I've covered the coastline in 50 walks, starting at Manningtree and ending at Rainham. Three Essex islands, Mersea, Canvey and Wallasea, are also included.

Many of the routes include inland sections, providing variation from the sea walls as they take the walker through the delightful Essex countryside and woodland. Some offer options of different length and most can be linked to form a longer route for the more ambitious walker.

Most walks follow circular routes, whilst some have an easy return to the start by train and three use summer ferries. Buses are less popular, although the Essex rural network has good reliability, and a few walks might best be done by parking at the end and taking a bus to the start. Some shorter walks are suited to being followed out and back by the same route (but of course with different views). I've suggested pubs for refreshment, although advise checking websites to confirm opening and food availability.

I've given information on parking but also public transport and would encourage walkers to leave their car behind if they can. As timetables change, I suggest using traveline.info to find bus and train times but have given an indication of frequency as follows:

Every 30 mins or less: Frequent

Every 30 – 60 mins: Regular

Roughly two hourly: Limited

Less than 2 hourly: Occasional

Each walk is accompanied with a map, which should be used in conjunction with the directions. Distances are shown in miles as this is what most walkers prefer, hence to avoid mixing units I've used the traditional yards not metres. You may find it helpful to also carry a larger scale 1:25,000 Ordnance Survey Explorer Map for extra detail.

I've made the instructions as detailed as reasonably practical without mentioning every gate, stile or side path on the route. Walkers should assume that the route stays on the same path or road, not taking turnings to left or right, unless stated. Sometimes distances could be shortened by using roads but other than quiet lanes, I've avoided these wherever possible.

Many of the routes cover quite isolated stretches of coast, some of the most remote in England, and walkers should ensure that they are suitably equipped before setting off. There is often little shelter from rain or sun. Possible problems to be aware of are high vegetation on some of the lesser used paths, particularly the more isolated sea walls in mid-summer before the grass is cut, although it's usually possible to avoid this by walking below the embankment. Some areas may be muddy in winter and I've noted a few that were particularly bad when I walked them. Sometimes paths aren't clear after a field has been ploughed and until the route becomes re-established it can be easier to walk around the edge of a field. Generally however walking is straightforward, often with long stretches of sea wall where the route is obvious, although it's still best to keep an eye on the map to know where you are. It is advisable to read through the full directions before you start.

Whilst most of the Essex coastline has remained unaltered for many years, there will inevitably be occasional changes, such as new areas of managed retreat. I will put these on my website, along with any comments from readers that might be helpful to other walkers (petercatonbooks.co.uk).

With views, atmosphere and wildlife changing according to season, tide and weather, the Essex estuaries are never the same and repeating the same walk many times will always bring new experiences. Whilst sunshine might be favoured, a dull or misty day, or an early morning, enhances the atmosphere of the enigmatic marshes. High tide brings water lapping close to the paths but as the sea recedes a host of birds appear to feast on the mud. The fortunate walker may see some of our more elusive mammals; deer, seals, water voles, hares, or even otters.

A few years ago I walked the whole length of the county's coast, writing Essex Coast Walk as a narrative of my walk, the people met, history, places and wildlife seen. It has been most enjoyable to revisit the whole coast in working out these fifty walks and gave the opportunity to update and reprint Essex Coast Walk. Often I met only a couple of others walking but found that the fewer the people seen, the more willing to chat they are. I hope that this book will encourage more to come out and enjoy the unique Essex coast.

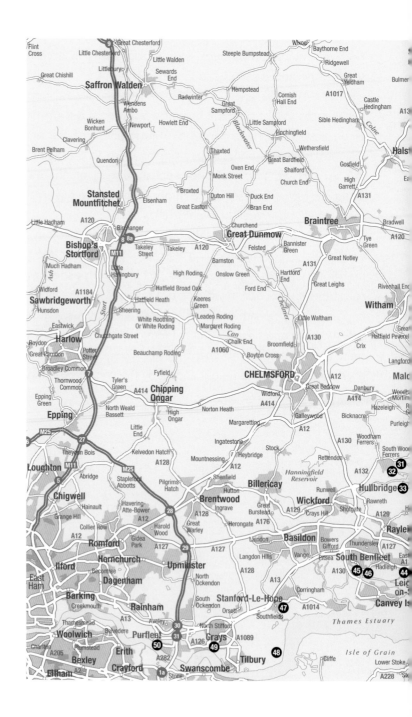

WALK 1

MANNINGTREE – MISTLEY & CIRCULAR
3½ / 7 MILES

A delightful and varied walk across countryside and along the River Stour to the historic village of Mistley, with the option to return by train, or on foot by an interesting route through old Manningtree & Lawford, enjoying some wonderful countryside and views.

Start – Manningtree station / Finish – Manningtree or Mistley stations

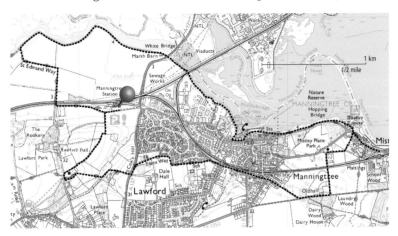

Parking: Manningtree & Mistley stations, Manningtree, Mistley
Train: Manningtree (frequent), Mistley (regular)
Bus: Manningtree (frequent), Mistley (regular)
Shops: Manningtree & Mistley
Refreshments: Cafés & pubs at Manningtree & Mistley
Public Toilets: Manningtree

In Tudor times Manningtree was a prosperous town, profiting from trade in wool and cloth, which were loaded onto sailing barges at the quay. Its relative prosperity and coastal position has resulted in various influences leaving a legacy of interesting and aesthetically pleasing buildings.

1. Turn right down the slope at the right of the station entrance and join a short length of footpath on the left of the large flat car park entrance, which soon meets a lane.

2. Turn right along the lane, then where this bends sharp left after 1/3 mile take a track on the right, passing under the railway.

3. Continue on the track which narrows to a path before reaching the embankment of the Stour. Turn right (left leads to Flatford Mill, a 1½ mile walk along the river bank).

4. Follow the embankment on what is a beautiful stretch of rural river, where birdlife abounds, reaching the White Bridge after a mile. Actually mainly blue, this forms the road boundary between Essex and Suffolk. Cross the road and continue on the path opposite towards a railway bridge.

The derelict industrial site across the river was once a huge plastics plant employing over 5,000 people. It is earmarked for housing development.

5. Pass under the railway, after which views open up along the estuary to Manningtree, Mistley & Felixstowe. The area of salt marsh to your left is Hogmarsh Island.

6. On reaching Manningtree it's necessary to leave the river for a short distance. Take the steps down at the end of the embankment, follow the path left to the road and turn left.

7. Pass The Skinners Arms then turn left onto North Street after 100 yards and left into South Street after 175 yards. (Alternatively for shops & cafes stay on High Street, which bends left back to the river after ½ mile). Continue by the river for ½ mile on what is known as The Walls.

The Stour here supports one of the largest herds of swans in the UK, although numbers have declined from the 700 who once lived off the washings from Mistley Maltings.

8. A stream is crossed on Hopping Bridge, once the site of some of the less savoury events in the town's history.

Manningtree was the home of Matthew Hopkins, the seventeenth century Witch Finder General. He used the traditional, if not entirely fair method to determine whether suspects were witches. The unfortunate women were 'ducked' in the river to ascertain whether they floated or sunk. Those who sunk and drowned were decreed as innocent. Those who floated were guilty, so hung, or burned at the stake.

9. The road bends inland soon passing Mistley Towers at the start of the village. These two towers are all that remains of what was once the magnificent church of St Mary the Virgin. Built in 1735, it was remodelled by the architect Robert Adam in 1771 at the commission of the wealthy local politician Richard Rigby who had ambitious plans to turn Mistley into a spa town. These however were thwarted when funds ran out after he was obliged to resign his position as Paymaster of the Forces, being unable to account for large sums of public money found in his possession.

10. A swan fountain in the village centre dates from Rigby's venture. To the left is Mistley Quay Workshops and café (open Wed – Sun) and on the right Mistley Thorne, a hotel dating from 1723, where Matthew Hopkins was said to have held some of his trials. For Mistley station continue a further 300 yards down the road.

11. If returning to Manningtree on foot take the short road to the right of Mistley Thorne which leads to an attractive green. Follow the path diagonally across the green and continue towards Mistley Church.

12. At the end of the churchyard turn left into Church Lane, which is followed under the railway to a T junction with another track (¼ mile). Turn right, entering a wood after a short distance. Immediately at the end of the wood (¼ mile from joining the track) take a narrow path on the right, initially between a fence and hedge, then houses, until meeting a road.

13. Cross the road and continue along the lane on the left fork, Barnfield, which leads to a short alleyway. At the next road turn right, then left after 25 yards along Mill Road, which runs parallel with the railway and passes interesting Victorian & Edwardian waterworks buildings.

14. Cross the next road and proceed along a path alongside playing fields. At the end of the school follow the path beside houses then continue straight on along a grassy path to the left of fruit trees (signed Essex Way), which drops down through Owl's Flight Dell, an attractive conservation area. Pass a pond then bear sharp left, taking a left fork where the path splits and ascending to the A137 road.

15. After 75 yards cross the road with care and take a track on the right. Manningtree railway station soon comes into view.

16. As the track bends left after 200 yards by a house, pass through a kissing gate on the right and take a grassy path running downhill by the edge of the wood. Pass through another gate, cross Wignall Brook and continue uphill across the field to the impressive St Mary's Church

Dating from the 14th century, St Mary's was linked to nearby Lawford Hall, which is probably why it stands in the countryside rather than the village centre.

17. Pass The Old School House then turn right on the lane, pass the 17th century Church Clerks Cottage and enter the churchyard. Take a path immediately on the left which runs under trees, leaving the churchyard through a gate on the left.

18. The path gently descends the hill with excellent views down the Stour estuary and to Suffolk. The pink building across the river is Stutton Mill. On reaching a lane turn right, then left after 50 yards to return to the station.

A 9½ mile walk from Manningtree to Wrabness can be made by linking from 10 with the start of Walk 2.

WALK 2

MISTLEY – WRABNESS & WRABNESS CIRCULAR
6 / 1½ MILES

A varied walk along the Stour valley, through countryside with good views of the estuary, then alongside the river. Most of the route is on the Essex Way long distance footpath and its signs can be followed, although they are not at every junction. Return to Mistley by train takes just five minutes. Alternatively a short circular walk around Wrabness, passing one of the most unusual houses in Essex.

Start – Mistley station/ Finish – Wrabness station
(Wrabness circular start from Wrabness station)

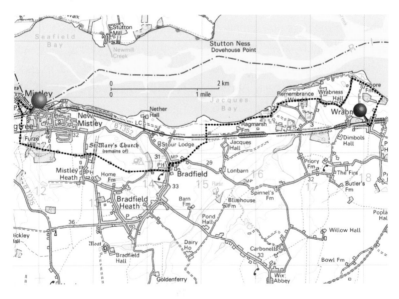

Parking: Mistley & Wrabness stations
Train: Mistley, Wrabness (regular)

Bus: Mistley, Wrabness (regular)
Shops: Mistley & Wrabness
Refreshments: Cafés & pubs at Mistley, pub at Bradfield, Community
Café atWrabness
Public Toilets: None

The pleasant village of Mistley is still active as a small port, as it has been since a quay was constructed in 1720. A Roman road to Colchester may have been built to serve a much earlier port. Unfortunately 500 years of public access to the quay was stopped by a controversial 'safety fence' erected amid scenes of public protest in 2008.

1. Turn left from Mistley station, heading the short distance into the village centre where the craft gallery, swan fountain and Mistley Towers can all be viewed. (See Walk 1).

2. Turn left onto The Green alongside Mistley Thorn, continuing to a brick wall where a path runs left behind the maltings. This soon bends sharp right and leads to steps under the railway.

Mistley's malting history dates from the late 19ᵗʰ century, when barley was turned into malt and shipped to London by Thames barges. Still active, the maltings now supply food products to many countries.

3. Immediately after the bridge go through a kissing gate and continue on the path across the middle of a field (a mass of buttercups in early summer). A good view emerges of the Victorian Mistley Church to the right.

4. Pass through two more kissing gates either side of a track, staying on the path which runs across the next field. At the end of the field don't go through the gate but turn left along a track which soon enters a wood, where it divides into three.

5. There are many paths within the wood so care is needed. Take the centre path which runs slightly uphill, then where this divides either side of a large tree select the left option. This runs alongside a line of old concrete fence posts before passing a rugby field and emerging from the wood.

6. The path continues across a field before meeting a road. Turn right along the road then pass through a gate to the footpath

on the left after 50 yards. This runs alongside a cottage, passes through another kissing gate and leads to a large field from where there are fine views of the Stour and to Suffolk.

7. Cross the next field, bearing left at the end to pass through a gap in the hedge. On reaching a lane turn left, soon reaching the village of Bradfield.

8. Turn left on the main road, passing St Lawrence Church, then take the road on the right opposite Strangers Home, a Victorian inn where refreshment may be sought.

9. Stay on the road for 300 yards, taking great care where there's no pavement on a sharp right bend. Part way round the bend take a footpath on the left which runs beside a hedge then across a field with superb views of the Stour.

10. The path runs almost to the railway line, then turns right alongside it, before passing left through a bridge. From here continue straight on across the field towards the river.

11. Turn right along the low embankment, dropping down to the river side of the wall just after a derelict barn and reaching the entrance to Wrabness Nature Reserve after a further 350 yards.

Now managed by Essex Wildlife Trust, this 60 acre reserve served as a naval mine depot and was owned by the MoD until 1963. Attempts to develop it, including plans to build a prison, were thwarted and in 1992 the land was purchased by local appeal to be kept as a nature reserve. It provides excellent habitat for a variety of birds and many butterflies, dragonflies and damselflies can be seen.

12. After entering the reserve take the left fork where the path splits after a few yards. Pass a wildlife hide and continue along the paved path, eventually taking a left fork signposted Essex Way. This goes down some steps and heads back towards the river.

13. On reaching an open paved area take the second path on the left. The sea wall is soon reached by a few steps.

14. Turn right along the embankment for a short distance then descend steps towards the end of the little bay. At low tide it's

possible to continue on the beach but this isn't easy walking so an inland route is recommended.

15. Take a path to the left of the steps (don't walk up the lane). The path runs between hedges, crosses a paved roadway and continues in a straight line gently uphill.

16. Turn right on meeting a track by a house, then left onto a road after a few yards. Pass a few houses then Wrabness Church.

The Norman All Saints Church is unusual in that its bell stands in the graveyard, having fallen to the ground in the seventeenth century. According to legend, each time the steeple was rebuilt the Devil came in the night and blew it down, so it was decided to hang the bell at ground level.

17. After the last building turn left down Stone Lane, passing a caravan site. The private sign applies only to vehicles. Turn right before a gate almost at the river, walking behind beach houses then onto an embankment.

18. On reaching a wood turn right, following the path as it ascends towards Wrabness village, passing Julie's House, one of the strangest buildings on the Essex coast.

Designed by Turner Prize winner Grayson Perry, 'A House for Essex' is intended to 'evoke a tradition of wayside and pilgrimage chapels in the landscape'. Perry says he was inspired by follies, eccentric homes, shrines and fairy tales and dedicated the house to a fictitious Julie. It's certainly not to everyone's taste and some of the locals would rather it had never appeared here above the Stour.

19. Continue as the path becomes a lane and crosses the railway. Wrabness station, Community Shop and Café are on the right.

WRABNESS CIRCULAR (1½ MILES)

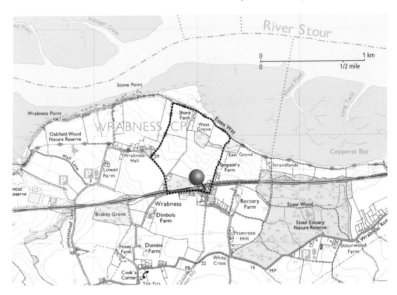

A. On leaving the station approach turn left down Black Boys Lane by Wrabness Community Shop & Café. Grayson Perry's remarkable house is soon reached

B. Continue on the path downhill to the Stour, then turn left on the riverside path. Follow the path for 0.4 miles, passing Shore Farm, until reaching a caravan site, then turn left up Stone Lane

C. At the top of the lane you may wish to go right on the road for a few yards to view All Saints Church, otherwise turn left along the quiet Church Road with good views down the Stour

D. After crossing a railway bridge turn left along Station Road, reaching Wrabness station in ¼ mile.

A 14 mile walk along the Essex Way from Mistley to Harwich can be made by staying on the sea wall at 18 and continuing from 2 of Walk 3.

WALK 3

WRABNESS – HARWICH INTERNATIONAL / HARWICH
5 / 9 MILES

Starting alongside the Stour, then heading inland through woods and countryside, this walk gives two choices for reaching the historic maritime town of Harwich. The shorter route uses part of one of the longest footpaths in Europe and terminates at Harwich International station, for return by train (or onward to Harwich on foot or train). The alternative route, which includes more coastal walking, follows the Essex Way alongside the North Sea to Dovercourt and Harwich, using directions from 11 of Walk 4.

Start – Wrabness station Finish / Harwich or Harwic
International stations

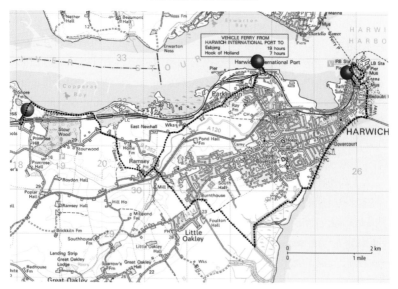

Parking: Wrabness station (charged) Harwich, Ramsey, Dovercourt
Train: Wrabness, Harwich, Harwich International, Dovercourt (all
regular)
Bus: Wrabness, Dovercourt, Harwich, Harwich International
Shops: Wrabness, Harwich, Dovercourt
Refreshments: Pubs at Harwich, Dovercourt, Ramsey. Cafés at
Wrabness, Harwich, Dovercourt
Public Toilets: Harwich, Harwich International Port, Dovercourt

1. On leaving the station approach turn left down Black Boy
   Lane by Wrabness Community Shop & Café. Grayson Perry's
   remarkable house is soon reached (see Walk 2).
2. Continue on the path downhill to the Stour, then turn right on
   the riverside path into East Grove Wood.
3. Pass through a pair of kissing gates and stay by the river until
   reaching Copperas Wood (part of Stour Wood, an RSPB
   reserve). Note that the path through the wood is not quite as
   shown on OS maps.
4. Cross a footbridge into the wood and take the left option as the
   path divides after a few yards. This gradually climbs away from the
   river, crosses a railway bridge and becomes a wider track through
   the Essex Wildlife Trust reserve. (By turning left at the bridge it's
   possible to walk two miles to hides by the river but not all the way
   to Harwich, so the route must divert further inland.)
5. Turn left on reaching Wrabness Road, follow this for ⅓ mile then
   take a footpath right. This runs along the edge of one field and
   straight over the next.
6. Pass through a gate in the hedge and turn left alongside horse
   paddocks, through a kissing gate and across a small field, coming
   out by Ramsey windmill.
*A common Suffolk design of post mill, Ramsey Mill originated at
Woodbridge and was moved here by boat in 1842. It last ground corn
in 1939 and was restored by volunteers in the 1970s.*
7. A short length of road leads to The Street, where a left turn
   takes you into the village of Ramsey.

SHORT ROUTE

8. Just after The Castle Inn turn left at a triangular junction onto Wrabness Road which is followed for 275 yards, passing The Lord Nelson. This closed in 1961, having been licensed since 1845, and also served as a post office.

9. At the end of the houses turn right onto a footpath (the first of two marked on the map). Follow this along the edge of one field and straight across the next, heading towards White Cottage.

10. Pass through the hedge and turn right along a track, which crosses a road after which it becomes a narrower path, then widens as it passes between a golf course and oil refinery.

11. This pleasant, easy walk is part of the E2 European Long Distance Path, a 3,000 mile route linking Galway with Nice.

12. On reaching a road go straight on for a short distance, then for Harwich International turn left into the port, following the designated walking route to the station.

LONG ROUTE

Turn right at the triangle by the Castle Inn at Ramsey and follow directions from 10 of Walk 4.

WALK 4

HARWICH CIRCULAR
12 / 9 MILES

A circular walk, incorporating an old railway line, part of the world's longest cycle route, crossing countryside using two long distance footpaths, following the sea wall passing Dovercourt and on to historic Harwich. If travelling by train the walk can be shortened by starting at Harwich International (6), or using the train for the Harwich International to Harwich section.

Start – Harwich Town or International stations, Ramsey or Dovercourt.

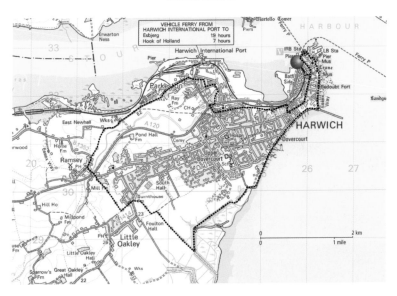

Parking: Harwich, Dovercourt, Ramsey
Train: Harwich, Harwich International, Dovercourt (regular)
Bus: Harwich, Harwich International, Dovercourt, Ramsey

Shops: Harwich, Dovercourt
Refreshments: Pubs at Harwich, Dovercourt, Ramsey. Cafés at
Harwich & Dovercourt
Public Toilets: Harwich, Harwich International Port, Dovercourt

1.   From Harwich Town station turn right along Main Road opposite
     the lighthouse, passing the entrance to Harwich Redoubt Fort,
     which was built to protect the town from Napoleonic invasion. On
     reaching Dovercourt after ⅔ mile turn right down Station Road.
2.   Turn left at the station, following a footpath parallel to the railway,
     with views of the river. This is part of the 6,000km North Sea Cycle
     Route, which runs through 8 countries from Bergen to Shetland.
3.   At the first three junctions stay on the paved path to the right, which
     straightens as it follows the old route of the railway to Harwich
     prior to diversion to the port when Parkeston Quay opened in
     1883. Stay on the railway path where the cycle route diverges to
     the right, reaching a roadway close to the Premier Inn after ¼ mile.
4.   Continue to Parkeston Road and turn right. Cross the busy A120
     to the right of the roundabout, turn left, then take an unsigned
     footpath on the right after 20 yards. After ~100 yards take a
     footpath on the left. This is Captain Fryatt's Riverside Walk.

A Harwich hero, Captain Charles Fryatt was in command of the SS Brussels when it was threatened by a U-boat who signalled for the British merchant ship to stop. Realising that his ship would be torpedoed, Fryatt attempted to ram the submarine before escaping. Despite being civilian non-combatant he was sentenced to death when captured a year later off the Netherlands.

5. On reaching the main road turn left, then follow the footpath as it runs through a park and into Garland Road. Turn right into Hamilton Street opposite Captain Fryatt pub, then left into Coller Road, continuing across a short pedestrian area at the end where old railway tracks can be seen.

6. Turn left along Station Road, or right for Harwich International (follow the walking route for ¼ mile to the station). If starting the walk from the station follow the walkway out of the port and turn right.

7. When the road divides after 250 yards bear left along Refinery Road. At the entrance to the refinery continue straight on along a gravel track running to the left of a fence. This narrows to a path after ½ mile at the end of the refinery. It is part of the E2 European Long Distance Footpath.

8. Cross a lane after ⅓ mile and continue a further 0.4 mile until reaching White Cottage. Pass through a gap in the hedge on the left opposite the house and follow the footpath across the field.

9. At the next field continue straight ahead to the right of the hedge, heading towards houses. Turn left at the road and on reaching a triangular road junction bear left.

The 18th century Castle Inn, the last of Ramsey's four pubs, is on the right. In 1979 it was the scene of a police shootout, when teenage gunman Paul Howe took over the pub after a high speed chase from Chelmsford. After wounding one officer Howe was shot dead by a police marksman as he tried to shoot his way to freedom.

10. The busy A120 is soon reached and crossed just to the left of the roundabout. Continue ahead up Church Hill, soon passing Ramsey War Memorial Hall.

11. Cross the road and take a footpath on the right adjacent to

Kingdom Hall. This is the Essex Way, which is now followed all the way to Harwich. The path soon crosses a footbridge and bears left up a hill, from which there is a good view of Ramsey, its mill and church.

12. Continue straight ahead on the left edge of a field, then between two open fields, heading towards houses. On meeting a paved path one field before the houses, turn left, soon passing Little Oakley Football Club.

13. Follow the roadway for 200 yards to the B1414. Cross the road, turn left, then take a footpath a few yards on the right.

14. Views soon open up towards the North Sea and Walton-on-the-Naze tower across Hamford Water. Bear right on meeting another path after 200 yards, then left at a wider path after a further ¼ mile.

15. After 150 yards descend steps on the right and follow a straight path which leads ¾ mile to the sea. Ascend the sea wall (close to a gate) and turn left towards Harwich.

16. Follow the path round the salt marsh of South Hall Creek, then by the sea at a grassy area, at the end of which is a car park. From here the promenade is followed for 2½ miles along Dovercourt seafront into Harwich.

Two cast iron lighthouses on Dovercourt beach were 'leading lights', which ships would keep lined up to follow the channel into Harwich. They were built to replace a pair of brick lighthouses in Harwich which became redundant in 1863 when the channel moved.

17. After 2 miles the promenade bends left under Beacon Cliff by a breakwater.

Above can be seen some of the military defences of Beacon Hill Fort, where Henry VIII built a blockhouse to protect his naval base, and more recently gun emplacements protected the port in both World Wars.

18. Harwich is now approached, with the port of Felixstowe across the river. Pass the Low Lighthouse, now a maritime museum and continue alongside a green at the end of which can be seen a treadmill crane. This was once used in the dockyard and operated by two men walking inside a wheel 'hamster style'.

19. At the end of the promenade turn left by the Lifeboat Museum then following signs for the quay, right after ~80 yards along Wellington Street, passing the Electric Palace, one of Britain's oldest purpose-built cinemas, dating from 1911.

20. Continue straight on along Kings Quay Street, passing The Globe, Harwich's oldest open pub, and Navyard Wharf where many fine naval ships were built, until reaching Ha'Penny Pier.

Opened in 1853, the pier's name originates from the ½d toll charged. The little ticket office is a charming example of late Victorian architecture. Paddle steamers once called here and a ferry still runs to Felixstowe and Shotley. A few fishing vessels use the area of water enclosed by the pier, a remnant of a once great 19th century fishing fleet.

21. Continue on the pavement by the harbour wall, then for the station turn left at the roundabout, passing to the left of Trinity House. The attractive station building is to the right of the High Lighthouse.

A link can be made with Walk 5 by turning right on the sea wall at 15.

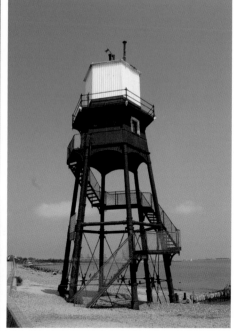

WALK 5

LITTLE OAKLEY CIRCULAR
5½ MILES

A circular walk with excellent views across Hamford Water. Abundant birdlife in this internationally important wetland can be seen from the sea wall.

Start – The Cherry Tree, Little Oakley

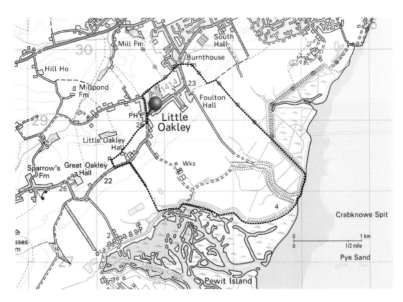

Parking: Street parking in Little Oakley (limited)

Train: Nearest is Dovercourt, then walk or bus

Bus: Little Oakley (regular)

Shops: None

Refreshments: Pub at Little Oakley

Public Toilets: None

1. From the Cherry Tree head up Rectory Road (signed Wrabness). Just after Old School House take a footpath on the right where the road bends left after 300 yards.
2. Follow the path as it runs behind houses then across a field from where there's a view to Ramsey Mill. Pass Little Oakley Football Club and follow the roadway for 200 yards, passing Little Oakley War Memorial, until meeting the B1414. Cross the road, turn left, then take a footpath (The Essex Way) 20 yards on the right.
3. Views soon open up towards the North Sea and Walton-on-the-Naze tower across Hamford Water. Bear right on meeting another path after 200 yards, then left at a wider path after a further ¼ mile.
4. After 150 yards descend steps on the right and follow a straight path which leads ¾ mile to the sea. Ascend the sea wall to the right of a gate and turn right along the embankment, which is followed for the next 2 miles.
5. After a short distance Irlam's Beach is reached and you are by the open sea. As the path bends right towards salt marsh there's no indication of the long detour needed to reach The Naze opposite.

The tidal creeks, mudflats, salt marsh and islands of Hamford Water are an internationally important wetland for birds and designated as a National Nature Reserve. It is on the migration route for many species and provides wintering grounds for brent geese, godwit, redshank, shelduck, teal and avocet and breeding grounds for terns. In addition, there are nationally important numbers of wigeon, pintail, ringed plover, curlew and dunlin.

6. Just beyond a small jetty by an area that at low tide seems appropriately named Bull's Ooze, a barbed wire fence blocks

the path. Signs make it clear that walkers cannot continue on the
sea wall to Bramble Island (not actually an island).

*These are no ordinary Private signs but warn of prosecution under the
Explosives Act. In 1905 Bramble Island was acquired by the Explosives
Company and a factory built to produce explosives. These were initially
taken by horse and cart to Thorpe-le-Soken station but as output
increased, the plant making a great contribution to the war effort, a
dock was constructed and barges used. Although there is no longer
manufacturing, Bramble Island is still used for the storage of explosives,
hence the signs and need for walkers to head inland.*

7.   Leave the sea wall by the signs and follow a track gently uphill
     towards an old church. On reaching Clacton Road opposite Little
     Oakley Hall turn left and proceed with care for 275 yards, then
     turn right along a track towards St Mary's House.

*Formerly a parish church, St Mary's was declared redundant in 1973
and converted to a house in the early 1980s. The nave dates from the
early 12th century and as a Listed building its many historic features have
been retained.*

8.   Turn right on the footpath in front of St Mary's and walk left of
     trees after 175 yards. Follow the path across two fields (ignoring
     two paths on left) until reaching the road after ½ mile. Turn left
     to the Cherry Tree (75 yards).

*As access to the sea wall is barred at Bramble Island, to link with Walk 6
it's necessary to follow roads and paths through Great Oakley.*

WALK 6

BEAUMONT QUAY – KIRBY-LE-SOKEN & KIRBY-LE-SOKEN CIRCULAR
4½ MILES (9 MILES OUT & BACK), 3 MILES CIRCULAR

A remote walk along the quiet banks of Hamford Water. Whilst there's no easy return to the start by public transport, there is the option of pub refreshment before walking back and enjoying views in the opposite direction. A short circular walk from Kirby-le-Soken, passing the attractive Kirby Quay, gives a taste of the enigmatic Hamford Water.

Start – Beaumont Quay / Finish – The Ship Kirby-le-Soken
(Kirby-Le-Soken Circular starts at The Ship, Walton Road)

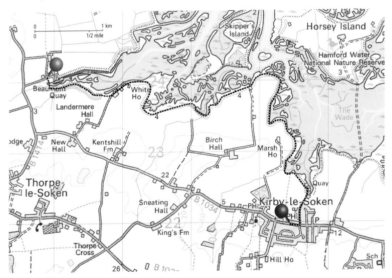

Parking: Beaumont Quay, Kirby-le-Soken (street parking)
Train: Closest are Thorpe-le-Soken or Kirby Cross, then walk or bus.
Bus: Beaumont (regular) & Kirby-le-Soken (frequent)

Shops: Kirby-le-Soken
Refreshments: Pubs at Kirby-le-Soken
Public Toilets: None

Beaumont Quay is reached along Quay Lane on the right of the B1414 Harwich Road between Kirby-le-Soken and Beaumont. There is a small parking area on the right towards the end of several farm buildings, from where a gate leads to the quay. Buses pass the start of the lane at Beaumont Bridge, but there are no official stops between the two villages.

1. Pass through the gate from the parking area, soon reaching Beaumont Quay.

Built in 1832 using stones taken from the old London Bridge, Beaumont Quay saw flourishing trade in the 19th century, once boasting a 600 tonne coal store, a large granary, limekiln and its own stables. The preserved lime kiln can still be seen.

2. Take the path on the left, soon passing the wreck of The Rose, originally a 42 tonne Thames sailing barge, which was later converted to a lighter and has lain here since the 1960s. Continue on the sea wall, until heading slightly inland to a row of cottages after ¾ mile.

The cottages, which were built by Richard Rigby, once included an inn called the Kings Head, which lost its licence in 1913 after becoming a notorious smugglers haunt. A plaque on one of the cottages tells that it was home to Sir William Gull, physician to Queen Victoria.

3. Follow the lane in front of the cottages, then take a path on the left leading to Landermere Quay and continue on the sea wall for the next 3½ miles.

To the left is Skipper's Island, an Essex Wildlife Trust reserve, for which the former 'walking route' is reached by a concrete barn after ~2 miles. Access by boat to this tidal island is permitted only by arrangement with the Trust and the causeway is no longer maintained as a safe route.

4. Approaching Kirby Quay the path runs inland of a small wooded area. Beyond the trees turn left through a gap and continue across or round a field, then cross a footbridge over a stream on the left. To the left is Quay House, a former granary on the quay and to the right the pretty Thatch Cottage.

5. Turn right along Quay Lane, reaching the main road in Kirby-le-Soken after ⅓ mile. The Ship, a 17th century pub, is 150 yards on the left and The Red Lion a further ¼ mile opposite St Michael's Church.

6. To return to Beaumont Quay follow the circular walk from (A), but instead of turning right at the end of the second field (B), go left through a gap in the hedge and rejoin the sea wall heading back to the start of your walk.

KIRBY-LE-SOKEN CIRCULAR (3 MILES)

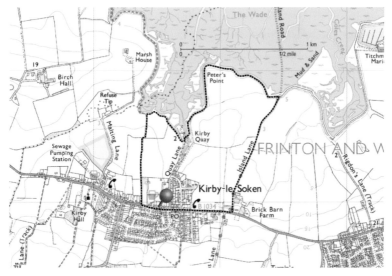

A. Facing The Ship, turn left along Walton Road, then after 75 yards take a footpath on the right. This runs initially between fences then along the right edge of a field, before switching to the left of the next field.

B. At the end of the field turn right in front of a hedge, soon reaching the sea. Stay to the right of the next hedge then pass through a gap on the left. Continue across or round the next field, then cross a footbridge on the left to the picturesque Kirby Quay.

Hamford Water was the setting for Arthur Ransome's Secret Water, in which Kirby Quay was called 'Witch's Quay', in the book the little wooden cottage, now Thatch Cottage, was Witch's Cottage. The Quay House was originally a granary and barges docked here, transporting coal, grain, sand, fertiliser and fish.

C. Turn left towards the Quay House, then right after 75 yards, passing behind wooden huts and crossing a dam. Note that this is covered for a short while on some high tides. Do not attempt to cross until the water recedes.

D. Turn left and follow the sea wall for almost a mile until reaching a slipway and jetty by a pill box. This is the slipway for Horsey Island and at low tide the mile long causeway can be seen stretching across the mud. The island, which has a history of racehorse breeding, is still farmed and the owners let a holiday cottage.

E. Turn right along Island Lane, reaching Walton Road after 0.6 miles. Turn right along the pavement, reaching The Ship after ½ mile.

Road walking is required to link with Walk 7, turning left along Walton Road at 5.

WALK 7

WALTON-ON-THE-NAZE CIRCULAR
6 MILES

A varied walk from a Victorian seaside town, along the rural creeks of Hamford Water, passing crumbling cliffs of great archaeological interest and an historic tower, returning along the seafront, or with the low tide option of beach walking.

Start – Walton-on-the-Naze Pier

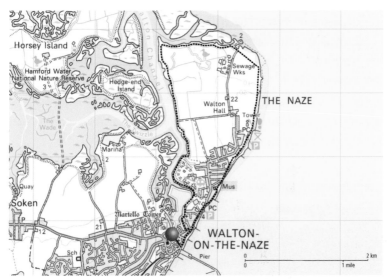

Parking: Walton-on-the-Naze town & The Naze
Train: Walton-on-the-Naze (regular)
Bus: Walton-on-the-Naze (regular)
Shops: Walton-on-the-Naze
Refreshments: Pubs & cafés at Walton-on-the-Naze & The Naze
Public Toilets: Walton-on-the-Naze & The Naze

The pier is reached by turning right out of the station and heading downhill for ¼ mile, or from the various car parks around the town.

1. Facing the sea, turn left from the pier. After ¼ mile turn left just before The Royal Albion, into Saville Street. Turn left into High Street after 60 yards, then right into North Street after 70 yards.
2. Continue as North Street runs through a paved area, reaching a small green. In the far corner of the green take a footpath that brings you onto the sea wall, which is followed for the next 3 miles.
3. A large chalet park is passed as you proceed along Walton Channel. Just before a wharf is a WW2 concrete barge (see Walk 50). Boat trips operate from the wharf to view seals in Hamford Water.
4. Passing The Twizzle, the channel feeding into the southern side of Hamford Water, the path (although not marked on all maps) continues with Walton Hall Marshes to the right and Hedge-End Island to the left. Trees further across the water are on Horsey Island.

At Cormorant Creek the path turns sharply to the right, following the creek for almost a mile until reaching the open sea. With appropriate care, at low tide it's possible to walk along the beach back to Walton-on-the-Naze, passing below crumbling fossil-rich cliffs.

More than 50 million years ago Essex was beneath a warm sea and as the cliffs erode fossils of sub-tropical marine life are revealed in the soft rock. Sharks teeth and carbonised wood are commonly found on the beach, particularly after stormy weather. Care should be taken if venturing close to the cliffs as erosion continues, illustrated by the WW2 pillboxes on the beach that once stood as lookouts high above.

5.   To follow the main route turn right along a paved pathway inland of a lagoon. A network of paths then lead towards the Naze Tower and grassy area on top of the cliffs. These may change as the sea claims more land but at the time of writing one of several routes was as follows.

6.   Stay on the embankment, passing a larger lagoon, then when the tarmac ends and the path has been eroded away, take the left of two grassy paths. This soon bears right away from the sea, passing through trees until the tower comes into sight.

The 85 foot octagonal brick-built Naze Tower was erected in 1721 by Trinity House as a navigational marker for the port of Harwich, a duty which it still performs today. Known locally as The Landmark, the tower was opened to the public for the first time in 2004. In summer months visitors can climb the spiral staircase and enjoy extensive views from the observation platform. Sea defences have recently been erected to protect the tower, which was built ¼ mile from the shore but now stands just 50 yards from the cliff edge.

7.   Passing to the left of the tower and through the car park, continue along a gravel road (Sunny Point) parallel with the sea.

8.   As the road bends right take a path on the left, heading almost back on yourself for a short distance as you descend to the beach. Turn right along the sea wall, passing many beach huts, before meeting the seafront road after ½ mile, which is followed back to the pier.

The walk can be extended to Clacton (13 miles) by linking with Walk 8.

WALK 8

WALTON-ON-THE-NAZE – FRINTON - CLACTON
2½ / 7 MILES

A classic and easy pier to pier walk between two famous Essex resorts, alongside open sea on hard promenades and sea walls. At low tide the first part of the walk can be done on sandy beaches. Option to break the walk at the exclusive town of Frinton-on-Sea.

Start – Walton-on-the-Naze Pier / Finish – Clacton Pier

Parking: Walton-on-the-Naze, Frinton, Clacton
Train: Walton-on-the-Naze, Frinton, Clacton (regular)
Bus: Walton-on-the-Naze, Frinton, Clacton (regular)
Shops: Walton-on-the-Naze, Frinton, Clacton
Refreshments: Pubs & cafés at Walton-on-the-Naze, Frinton, Clacton
Public Toilets: Walton-on-the-Naze, Frinton, Clacton

Alternatively park at Thorpe-le-Soken station, take the train to Walton-on-the-Naze and back from Clacton.
The pier is reached by turning right out of the station and heading downhill for ~¼ mile, or from the various car parks around the town.

1. Facing the sea, turn right from the pier walking along the concrete promenade which is lined with beach huts almost all the way to Frinton.
2. After 1¾ miles steps by a shelter (close to a slipway) lead up to Frinton. To visit this unique town climb the steps, cross a greensward and continue directly ahead onto Connaught Avenue opposite. This is Frinton's main street. The town is ¼ mile from the sea and the station, from where a train can be taken back to Walton, a further ½ mile along the same road.

Whilst not quite as exclusive as its reputation, Frinton-on-Sea retains a genteel nature and with a large retired population there is perhaps some truth in the old music hall joke 'Harwich for the Continent, Frinton for the incontinent'. Connaught Avenue retains a good selection of independent shops, plus the Lock and Barrel, the town's only pub, which opened amidst much opposition in 2000.

3. For Clacton stay on the sea wall, climbing a few steps at the end of Frinton's large greensward and continuing past beach huts which stand on wooden stilts on the beach.
4. For almost a mile the exclusive Frinton Golf Club is to your right, after which is a gate into Holland Haven Nature Reserve and a path which can be followed as a diversion through the reserve.

Holland Haven's 100 acres of mostly grazing marsh and lagoons supports a wide variety of wildlife including ruddy darter dragonfly and larger carder bee. Over 200 bird species have been recorded here.

5. Approaching a radar tower (which monitors shipping entering the Thames estuary) follow a track as is rises slightly away from the beach. From the headland Clacton Pier can now be seen, somewhat deceptively still 3 miles away.

6. From here there is a choice of walking, either on the quieter promenade by the beach or a paved path on the cliff top, passing Holland-on-Sea. If the tide is high and sea rough the lower path is best avoided.

Clacton has been popular as a watering place since Victorian times, although has a history far beyond this. The beach is one of the oldest known sites of human habitation in the UK, a 400,000-year-old spearhead having been found in the cliffs along Marine Parade. Bones of woolly mammoths, lions, elephants and giant oxen tell of the former residents who drank from the Thames which once flowed here. The pier opened in 1871 and trippers arrived in their droves, initially by boat then train, with theatres and operetta houses built to attract the more discerning visitor.

7. On reaching Clacton, for the town centre cross Marine Parade immediately opposite the pier and head up a pedestrianised street. Bear right up Station Road for the railway station which is ½ mile from the pier.

The walk can be extended to Point Clear or St Osyth (14½ / 15½ miles) by linking with Walk 9.

WALK 9

CLACTON – ST OSYTH OR POINT CLEAR
8½ / 7½ MILES

A walk by the open sea and marshes, passing some isolated settlements, with options to finish at the villages of either St Osyth or Point Clear, from both of which regular buses return to Clacton. An alternative is an out and back walk to Colne Point Nature Reserve, which can be shortened by starting from car parks at Seawick or Jaywick.

Start – Clacton Pier / Finish – St Osyth or Point Clear villages

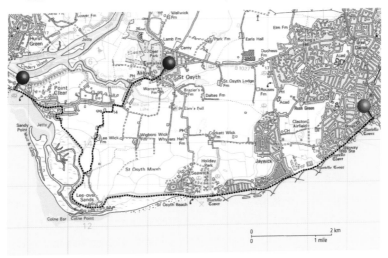

Parking:: Clacton, Jaywick, Seawick, St Osyth, Point Clear
Train: Clacton (regular)
Bus: Clacton, Jaywick, St Osyth, Point Clear (regular)
Shops: Clacton, Jaywick, St Osyth
Refreshments: Clacton, Jaywick, Seawick, St Osyth, Point Clear
Public Toilets: Clacton, Jaywick, St Osyth

1. Facing the sea turn right at Clacton Pier, heading along the promenade by the sandy beach. Just after the lifeboat and Coastguard stations and the first of several Martello Towers on this walk, the paved path passes Martello Bay, which protected by dunes and breakwaters, is a popular area for water sports.

Inspired by a round fortress in Corsica that the British Navy unsuccessfully attacked in 1794, 103 Martello Towers were built during the Napoleonic Wars. Most were on the South East coast, with many in Essex and Suffolk. They would typically have housed a garrison of 15 – 25 men.

2. 1½ miles from Clacton and just after the golf course, the village of Jaywick is reached. The path stays by the sea but you may wish to divert inland to view the unusual village or use its facilities. (The public toilets at the east end of the town are summer only, but those at the west open all year).

Once a small farming community, Jaywick became a holiday village when London businessman Frank Stedman bought the land in 1928 and built 2,000 chalets. Despite council rules forbidding permanent occupancy, many soon became homes and Jaywick a small town. With high unemployment and poor housing it is one of Britain's most deprived neighbourhoods. Inundation by the 1953 Great Flood cost the lives of 37 Jaywick residents.

3. The path disappears for ½ mile from the village centre, so continue on the quiet road by the beach, with interesting views of Jaywick's chalets and side roads. Stay by the sea at the end of the village, following the path past another Martello Tower (housing a heritage exhibition) and Martello Beach Holiday Park.

4. The settlement of Seawick, comprised almost solely of caravans and chalets, is soon reached. This section of coast has the highest concentration of static holiday homes in the whole of Essex.

5. When the chalets finally come to an end the sea wall becomes grass covered as it runs between salt marsh and the expanse of St Osyth Marsh, reaching the isolated settlement of Lee-Over-Sands, 4½ miles walking from Clacton.

6. Colne Point Nature Reserve can be accessed by turning left down the roadway, otherwise continue straight on along the sea

wall as it runs inland of a large area of salt marsh.

The best developed spit on the Essex coast, Colne Point forms a 683 acre reserve comprising mainly of shingle ridge and salt marsh. It is an important nesting site for little terns. Access is no longer restricted to permit holders but visitors should respect fencing and notices to prevent seasonal disturbance to nesting birds. Note that areas around the car park and footbridge flood at high tide.

7. If heading for St Osyth take a path across a field on the right just after a sewage works. Turn left on reaching a lane and follow this for a mile, passing Lee Wick Farm and coming out on Point Clear Road. There is a bus stop opposite, from where regular buses return to Clacton. Alternatively turn right and follow the road for 1 mile into St Osyth.

8. Whilst not signed or shown on the OS map, a reasonable path exists on or below the sea wall towards Point Clear. 75 yards before the embankment path ends in bushes go through a gap in the hedge on the right, over a footbridge and along the edge of a field.

9. On reaching houses turn left down the road and follow Dumont Avenue as it bends right. Beacon Heights road is private but take the next left, Beacon Way, then turn left as this meets Point Clear Road.

10. Where the road bends right, with a first view of the River Colne, take a footpath between bollards on the left, which soon reaches the sea at Point Clear Bay. Regular buses return to Clacton from the end of Point Clear Road, which is reached by turning right at the start of the bay.

A further option (extra 4 miles) is to continue along the sea wall then follow the start of Walk 11 to St Osyth.

WALK 10

ST OSYTH CIRCULAR
2 / 6 MILES

A short walk around Mill Dam Lake at St Osyth, or a longer walk continuing to Point Clear and returning along the banks of creeks.

Start – The Quay, St Osyth

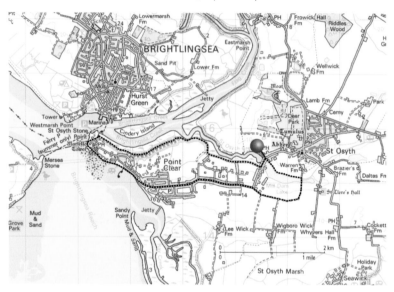

Parking: Mill Street Car Park St Osyth Quay, Point Clear
Train: Nearest is Clacton, then bus
Bus: St Osyth, Point Clear (regular)
Shops: St Osyth, Point Clear
Refreshments: Pubs & cafés & St Osyth & Point Clear
Public Toilets: None on route

1. Cross the road from Mill Street Car Park and follow a footpath along the left (east) bank of Mill Dam Lake.

There was a tidal mill by the creek from at least the 15th century. The last was built around 1730 and when it closed in 1930 the owner endeavoured to make a living from the premises, trying a tea room, boat hire, fish farming and even charging locals to skate on the frozen lake. The mill was demolished after losing its roof to a gale in 1962.

2. At the end of the lake (½ mile) take a track on the right running between the main lake and Reed Pond. After ¼ mile turn right onto a track which runs to the left of a hedge.

3. Continue straight on where this meets a lane after ¼ mile and follow this for 600 yards to Point Clear Road.

4. For the short walk turn right, following the road for 650 yards back to the dam. For the longer walk turn left, following Point Clear Road for 1¼ miles as it descends towards the sea.

5. As the road bends right just after Colne View Road take a footpath between bollards on the left, soon reaching the sea at Point Clear Bay by Rose Cottage, which has a large ship's bell standing outside. Just across the water is Sandy Point, the tip of Colne Point Nature Reserve.

6. Follow the paved path above the beach (more attractive at high tide than low), then by chalets and past a Martello Tower, until reaching a headland from where there are good views across

the water to Brightlingsea (right) and Mersea Island (ahead).

7.   The path turns sharp right, heading up Brightlingsea Creek, then after a mile bends right along St Osyth Creek for a further mile. On reaching the road turn left across the dam to return to the start.

In the middle of Brightlingsea Creek is Cindery Island, which contains many oyster pits. Another smaller island lies downstream. Until around 200 years ago these were joined but became separated by tides flowing from St Osyth Creek, apparently assisted by the owner of St Osyth Priory cutting away part of the island to allow easier access for his yacht.

WALK 11

BRIGHTLINGSEA – POINT CLEAR - ST OSYTH CIRCULAR
10 MILES

A circular walk mostly along the banks of creeks, using the Brightlingsea to Point Clear summer ferry.

Start – Brightlingsea Harbour (Town Hard) for ferry

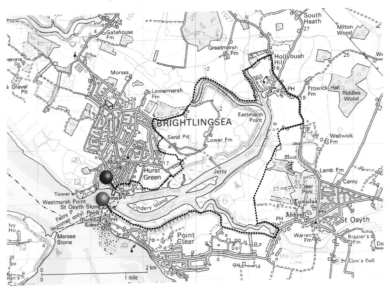

Parking: Brightlingsea

Train: Nearest is Wivenhoe, then bus

Bus: Brightlingsea, Point Clear, St Osyth (all regular)

Shops: Brightlingsea, St Osyth (off route)

Refreshments: Pubs & cafés at Brightlingsea, Point Clear, St Osyth

Public Toilets: Brightlingsea

The summer foot ferry from Brightlingsea to Point Clear (and East Mersea) takes just 3 minutes for a journey that is 10 miles by road. http://www.brightlingseaharbour.org/ferry.php

1. From the ferry at Point Clear turn left (facing inland), heading up Brightlingsea Creek for ~ 1 mile. The path then bends right along St Osyth Creek, reaching the road after a further mile.

2. Turn left across the dam, then follow a footpath on the left between Old Mill Cottage and a boatyard, which takes you back to the bank of St Osyth Creek after 200 yards.

3. In ¼ mile take a path on the right which runs up a gentle slope on the right of a field. Soon there are good views to Brightlingsea (left) and St Osyth Priory (right).

Dating from the 12th century, St Osyth Priory was one of the largest monasteries in Essex. Its many listed buildings and large park are now privately owned. The picturesque gatehouse stands just back from the road into St Osyth village.

4. Continue straight on when the path divides after ¼ mile and pass through a gate into Howlands Marsh Nature Reserve. Turn left on reaching a track after ½ mile, then after 125 yards go through a gate to a path into the edge of Nun's Wood.

5. After 350 yards pass through a gate on the left into Martins' Farm Country Park.

A former site of gravel extraction, this area was used for landfill for 30 years, but opened as a country park in 2008. It affords excellent views towards Brightlingsea and of the industrial archaeology of Wellwick Wharf.

6. Follow the path for ½ mile as it runs around the park, until reaching the access road (adjacent to car park). Unfortunately there is no exit at the north end of the park, so coastal walkers have to leave it here and turn left along the main road.

7. The Creek (formerly the Flag Inn) is passed after ½ mile. After a further ½ mile, just beyond a row of terrace cottages, take a path on the left. At the end of garden fences this bends left into a wood, soon emerging onto the sea wall at the head of Flag Creek.

8. Turn right, walking on the embankment for 1¾ miles to the head of the easterly branch of Flag Creek, then take a path on the right into a small wood. This soon joins a track passing between Marsh Farm House and a small lake.

9. Follow the track as it passes above a larger lake, then take a path on the left between fences at the end of the lake. On reaching a road turn left, then after 100 yards take a path running between houses on the right.

10. Turn left where this meets another path and continue by garden fences until emerging onto scrubland. Stay on the path across this and as it bears right into a newly wooded area.

11. Descend steps by a pond, coming out on Mill Street by East End Green Farm. Turn right, then after 25 yards left onto a short path to the creek. Follow the path as it runs beside salt marsh and disused oyster pits, then close to the river.

Ahead is Brightlingsea's small commercial port. Vessels based here support the Gunfleet Wind Farm off Clacton. It came to national attention in 1995 when thousands demonstrated against live animals being shipped abroad for slaughter.

12. As the path runs inland of a boatyard follow it to a gap in the left corner of the field. Turn left where this meets Lime Street and left again at Tower Street. At the end of the road turn left then immediately right to reach the quay.

WALK 12

BRIGHTLINGSEA CIRCULAR
6½ MILES

A circular walk along an old railway track on the banks of the beautiful River Colne and Alresford Creek, returning across farmland and through woods, with views across the river to Mersea Island.

Start – Brightlingsea Promenade

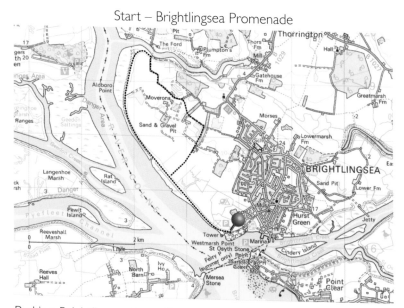

Parking: Brightlingsea town & promenade
Train: Nearest is Wivenhoe, then bus
Bus: Brightlingsea (regular)
Shops: Brightlingsea
Refreshments: Pubs Brightlingsea, cafés Brightlingsea town & promenade
Public Toilets: Brightlingsea town & promenade

1. Turn right from the town / car park, following the sea wall past lines of beach huts and an outdoor swimming pool, to Westmarsh Point. Here there is a paddling pool, café and an intriguing folly, Bateman's Tower.

The tower was built in 1883 by John Bateman as a recuperation area for his daughter who was suffering from consumption. Its roof was dismantled during WW2 when the tower was used as an observation post for the Royal Auxiliary Observer Corps, but reinstated in 2005 thanks to Heritage Lottery support. The tower is used by local yacht clubs for administration of sailing races.

2. Join the path which runs behind the café and onto the embankment alongside the river. This was once the Wivenhoe to Brightlingsea railway, which closed in 1962.

Mersea Island is seen across the water. Rat Island, a nature reserve with one of the largest colonies of black headed gulls in Essex, can be picked out in front of a large area of marshland. Grazing marshes to the right are part of Colne Estuary National Nature Reserve.

3. After about a mile the path passes through a gate before continuing along the river bank to Alresford Creek. The stub of embankment at the head of the creek once took the railway to a bridge.

4. Follow the path as it bends right up the picturesque creek. The OS map shows the path crossing a ford but this must not be attempted. Many people have got stuck in the mud here, so with no path on this bank it's necessary to head away from the water.

5. Turn right at a gate by the 'ford', heading along a winding gravel track. Where this meets a wider gravel road after ¾ mile, turn left.

6. After 175 yards the road reaches gravel workings and becomes metalled, at which point take a footpath on the right, which soon crosses a field with a good view over a lake to All Saints Church.
    Dating from around 1250, with its hill top position and 15th century tower, All Saints Church is one of the finest in East Anglia and a landmark for walkers for many miles.

7. Pass through a gate and cross a quarry road, joining a narrow path that runs above lakes. There are fine views across the Colne to Mersea.

8. The path comes out at the junction of several paths and tracks. Ignore the sign instructing to take the footpath towards the main road and follow a small path that starts next to where the one you arrived on emerges and heads back almost the same way. This is a Permissive Path.

9. Follow the path as it passes through Long Plantation and descends to the river, which it reaches by the gate passed through earlier. Return to Brightlingsea along the sea wall.

To link with Walk 13, making a 10½ mile walk to Wivenhoe including a 4 mile diversion around the head of Alresford Creek, at 6 stay on the road for ¾ mile until reaching the B1029 at Brightlingsea Hall. Turn left by the church, and after ⅔ mile take a footpath on the left leading to Thorrington Tide Mill.

WALK 13

WIVENHOE - ALRESFORD CREEK - THORRINGTON MILL CIRCULAR
CIRCULAR WALKS 3½, 5½, 6½ MILES
8 MILES TO THORRINGTON MILL AND BACK

A walk to the picturesque Alresford Creek along inland paths with fine views of the Colne valley, returning along river walls. There are three options for different lengths of circular walk, plus an extension to Thorrington Mill.

Start – Wivenhoe Quay

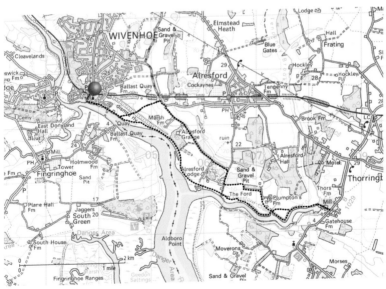

Parking: Wivenhoe
Train: Wivenhoe (regular)
Bus: Wivenhoe (regular

Shops: Wivenhoe
Refreshments: Pubs & cafés in Wivenhoe
Public Toilets: Wivenhoe

The quay is reached by heading down High Street from the car park or railway station.

The attractive town of Wivenhoe has many buildings of interest and much of the lower town is a conservation area. Its history is mainly of fishing, ship building and smuggling and it's said that many of the quayside houses had hidden spaces for concealing tobacco, silk and brandy.

1. Turn left facing the river and follow it upstream along the riverside path, passing the Colne Barrier, which was built in 1994 to protect from tidal surges and has been used far more often than predicted.

2. Join an earth embankment then take a path on the left after 100 yards. This heads inland, crosses the old Brightlingsea railway, then climbs gently, reaching a road after ½ mile.

3. Cross the road to walk (right) on the wide verge, then back again after 150 yards, turning right onto a paved track running to the right of the quarry road. There are good views across the Colne valley.

4. Continue straight on at the entrances to Marsh Farm and Alresford Grange, after which the track becomes a path running through trees. For the shortest circular walk (3½ miles) take the path on the right after ¼ mile which runs back to the river, where a right turn takes you back to Wivenhoe.

5. Continue straight on at the entrance to Alresford Lodge, then turn right on Ford Lane (not into the quarry) after ¼ mile.

6. Pass a lake on the left and take an unsigned footpath on the left opposite a house at the end of quarry buildings. For the 5½ mile circular continue along the lane, turn right at Alresford Creek and follow the riverbank path back to Wivenhoe.

7. There is a good view of Alresford Creek and All Saints Church as the path runs above a lake then alongside a wood, before joining a track and heading right towards the creek.

8. Where the track bends left just before derelict farm buildings,

take a path on the right, which meets the river wall at a small inlet after 200 yards. For the 6½ mile circular walk turn right along the embankment and follow the river wall back to Wivenhoe.

9. To continue a further ⅔ mile to Thorrington Mill, turn left inland along a path which rejoins the river wall after ¼ mile, then follow the embankment to the mill, crossing the millpond dam. Brightlingsea Road can be reached by walking past the mill and up the driveway.

The picturesque three storey timber-framed mill was built in 1831 and operated until 1926. Its fully restored machinery still grinds corn on occasional open days, powered by water released from the millpond, making it one of the few remaining working tide mills in the UK.

10. To return to Wivenhoe retrace your steps across the dam, pass through the gate on the left and rejoin the path along the bank of Alresford Creek.

11. Stay on the river wall, turning left over a footbridge after 0.4 mile, eventually reaching Alresford Ford. After a short stretch of road the path rejoins the river wall, which is followed to the end of the creek.

Running up the hill to Alresford Quarry is a line of rusting towers from a cable system which once took buckets of sand from the quarry, emptying them into barges. The substantial remains of the wharf still stand in the creek.

12. On reaching the main River Colne the path turns right, following the old railway line, first through trees then along open river bank to Wivenhoe.

13. Stay on walkways by the river until just beyond The Nottage Maritime Institute, a training centre and museum founded using a trust fund left by Captain Charles Nottage in 1896, then turn right into the town.

WALK 14

WIVENHOE – HYTHE – ROWHEDGE (CIRCULAR WITH FERRY)
5 MILES (3½ MILES TO HYTHE)

A walk on hard paths along the picturesque River Colne, with the option to return by train from Hythe or continue to Rowhedge along the opposite bank and the possibility of completing a circle by ferry on summer weekends (subject to tides). The route can easily be followed in reverse or started at Rowhedge if this fits better with ferry times.

Start – Wivenhoe Quay

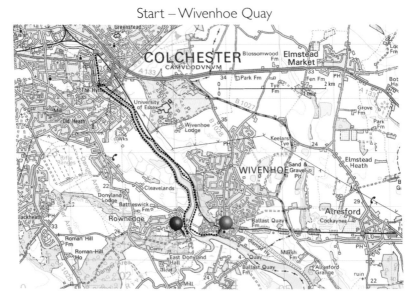

Parking: Wivenhoe, Hythe, Rowhedge
Train: Wivenhoe, Hythe (regular)
Bus: Wivenhoe, Hythe, Rowhedge (regular)
Shops: Wivenhoe, Hythe, Rowhedge

46

Refreshments: Pubs at Wivenhoe, Hythe, Rowhedge. Cafés at Wivenhoe
Public Toilets: Wivenhoe

Limited service summer ferry (www.rowhoeferry.co.uk). Timetables from Wivenhoe Books (www.wivenhoebooks.com).
The quay is reached by heading down High Street from the car park or railway station, passing St Mary the Virgin Church.

1. Facing the river, turn right passing in front of houses and along West Quay.
Wivenhoe's most attractive waterfront was once a hive of activity with docks, shipbuilding and fishing based here. Until the Colne was widened in the late 19th century Wivenhoe was effectively a port for Colchester and most of the town's population worked on the river.

2. As the quay ends turn left onto a footpath on the embankment. Opposite is the village of Rowhedge, where your walk ends. The path is followed to Hythe.

3. Bear left on meeting a wider path at the start of Wivenhoe Wood. Several seats by the path make excellent spots to sit and watch the river.

4. Continuing close to the water, the grey 1960s towers of Essex University are passed before reaching modern accommodation blocks. At the end of the buildings follow a short path to the road.

5. For Hythe station cross the road and continue on a riverside path for ~¾ mile, turning right onto the road for a few yards at the next road bridge. If preferred the Town to Port Trail can be followed into Colchester.

6. For Rowhedge turn left, crossing Colne Causeway Bridge, then at the roundabout take a walkway immediately left, which takes you back down to the river at Hythe Quay, now heading downstream on the opposite bank.

Built by the Normans around 1130, despite difficulties with the shallow river requiring frequent dredging, Hythe Quay was an important port, with both coastal and continental trade. By 1637 there was a weekly service to London, and with steam replacing sail in the 1830s, the journey time was reduced to just 7 hours. In 1892 3,000 vessels (mainly Thames sailing barges) used the dock and it remained busy into the latter part of the 20th century.

7. Stay on the quay which narrows to a path after ~½ mile, passing T.S. Colne Light, a steel lightship, launched at Dartmouth in 1954 and now a base for the Colchester Sea Cadets.

8. Pass through a gate into Hythe Lagoons, a 17 acre nature reserve based around old dredging lagoons, and continue along the path to Rowhedge.

9. On reaching Rowhedge take a footpath on the left which runs in front of houses (Thanet Walk) and emerges on a green by The Anchor. The ferry runs from a small jetty by the green.

10. For buses turn right across the green then right on the road, passing The Old Custom House. Follow the road as it bends left into Head Street where the bus stop is found after 50 yards.

If the ferry is running, the walk can be extended by 2½ miles by continuing to Fingringhoe following Walk 15.

WALK 15

WIVENHOE – ROWHEDGE – FINGRINGHOE CIRCULAR
2½ MILES

A circular walk along the picturesque Roman River and quiet lanes, using the Colne Ferry to and from Wivenhoe.

The ferry runs on summer weekends and Bank Holidays with timings according to the tide. Rowhedge is served roughly 1¾ hours and Fingringhoe 1 – 1½ hours either side of high tide. Note that until a jetty is built it may be necessary to walk on mud and paddle to board the ferry at Fingringhoe. The walk can easily be done in either direction. Advice on latest return times should be sought from the ferry skipper.

Start – Wivenhoe Quay

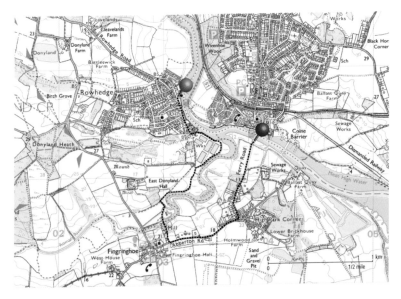

Parking: Wivenhoe, Rowhedge
Train: Wivenhoe (regular)
Bus: Wivenhoe, Rowhedge (regular)
Shops: Wivenhoe, Rowhedge
Refreshments: Pubs Wivenhoe, Rowhedge, Fingringhoe. Cafés
Wivenhoe
Public Toilets: Wivenhoe

*Limited service ferry (www.rowhoeferry.co.uk) Timetables from Wivenhoe
Books (www.wivenhoebooks.com)*
*To reach the quay walk down High Street. The ferry quay is by a shelter
outside the Nottage Institute.*

1. Turn left on disembarking from the ferry at Rowhedge, walk
    along the green then the lane inland of The Anchor.
*Rowhedge has a nautical history going back 2,000 years, when the
Romans established a supply base here, the Emperor Claudius landing
in AD43, bringing with him a number of elephants, who acted both
as beasts of burden and to scare the enemy. From Roman times until
comparatively recently Rowhedge acted as an out-port for Colchester,
unloading those vessels too large to make it further up the river. The last
cargo vessel arrived in 1999 and since then the quay and shipyard have
become derelict.*

2. When the lane ends after ¼ mile take a path on the left heading
    back to the river. Stay by the river as you walk on the edge of the
    old dock area. There are good views across the Colne to Wivenhoe.

3. Join a narrow path at the end of the paved dock area. This soon bends right heading up Roman River. At the head of the creek the path passes Fingringhoe Mill (now a private house) from where a lane is followed uphill.

Originally a Tudor tidal mill, Fingringhoe Mill was converted to steam in the 1800s and later to oil. It was active until the mid 1990s, producing mainly flaked maize for animal feed, as a condition of sale around 1931 was that flour was not to be milled in competition to the seller's other local mills.

4. Turn left on reaching a T junction, or right for a short (¼ mile) detour to visit the beautiful St Andrew's Church and The Whalebone Inn, but remember to keep an eye on the time for the return ferry.

Records show that the inn, which used to display the decaying jawbones of a whale as its sign, dates from at least 1735. Between the inn and church stands the Fingringhoe Oak, which with a girth of 7 metres and at least 600 years old, is claimed to be the oldest in Essex. According to legend it grew from an acorn placed in a buried smuggler's mouth.

5. Follow the lane downhill for ~½ mile, then opposite the bus stop turn left down Ferry Road which runs to the river. The ferry picks up at a line of posts at the foot of the slipway. Wave to attract the crew's attention as Fingringhoe is only served by request.

Other than Fingringhoe Wick Nature Reserve (which is well worth a visit) there is very limited coastal access on this section of the Colne and to reach Mersea Island it is necessary to head inland on paths and roads.

WALK 16

MERSEA ISLAND CIRCULAR
6 / 13 - 14½ MILES

A varied walk around the perimeter of Mersea Island, which with open sea, creeks, salt marshes and a working harbour, forms a microcosm of the Essex coast. At low tide much of the southern section can be walked on the beach, however instructions describe the high tide route. The total distance therefore varies a little according to the route chosen. A shorter option goes around the west end of the island, passing an ancient burial mound and the harbour.

Start – West Mersea village or Victoria Esplanade (2) where there is more parking space

Parking: West Mersea village, Victoria Esplanade, harbour
Train: Closest is Colchester, then bus
Bus: West Mersea (regular), East Mersea (occasional)

Shops: West Mersea
Refreshments: West Mersea village, by beaches & harbour
Public Toilets: West Mersea, Victoria Esplanade, harbour, Cudmore Grove

England's largest tidal island, Mersea is regularly cut off from the mainland when The Strood causeway is covered for a short period at high tide. The island was used by the Romans, who found its oysters which are still farmed today. Latterly Mersea has been 'discovered' and become a popular destination for visitors enjoying its excellent seafood.

1. From the centre of West Mersea village by St Peter & Paul Church, head downhill along Coast Road then after 200 yards take a footpath on the left to Monkey Beach.

2. Turn left, walking along the beach. Victoria Esplanade car parks are reached after 1 mile, after which you pass a long line of Mersea's famous pastel coloured beach huts.

3. Leave the beach at the end of the huts, turning left for the short route (follow from A), or joining a path above the sea wall to continue the full circuit of Mersea.

4. After ~½ mile, at the end of a caravan park follow the path to the left of trees, reaching East Mersea Youth Camp after ¼ mile. The sea wall was badly eroded in 2014 and until repaired a diversion inland is required, adding about 1 mile to the route.

5. Diversion - Follow a path to the left of the Youth Camp, leading to a lane close to Mersea Island Vineyard. Immediately after Rewsalls Farm turn right onto a footpath. After ~1 mile turn right opposite the beautiful East Mersea Church, where the Rev. Sabine Baring Gould was once rector, entering Cooper Beach Holiday Park. Continue straight on along a track through the holiday park to the sea wall, then turn left.

6. Continue on a hard path in front of chalets, then for a further ¼ mile until a sign shows the footpath heading inland. It's possible to stay on the beach at low tide but otherwise follow the well signed route by a holiday park, meeting Fen Lane after ¼ mile.

7. Follow the lane for ¼ mile, turn right on reaching East Road, then right after 75 yards into Broman's Lane. Follow the lane

into Cudmore Grove Country Park, where there is a small Information Room with light refreshments at weekends.

Cudmore Grove, an area rich in bird, wild flower and insect life, contains the only cliffs on Mersea. Fossils of bear, monkey, bison and straight tusked elephant, who lived here 300,000 years ago, have been found in the sandy deposits. Between the wars Cudmore Grove was part of a golf course but it never re-opened after defence use in WW2.

8. Follow a sign to the beach opposite the Information Room, crossing a meadow and regaining the sea wall to the left of low cliffs. Continue along a paved path, soon reaching the island's easterly tip. A summer ferry runs to Brightlingsea opposite.

9. From here the walk's character changes, as you follow the banks of the River Colne, then bend left after ½ mile, heading up Pyefleet Channel, soon passing Colchester Oyster Fishery.

10. The 2½ miles on the sea wall alongside Reeveshall & Maydays Marshes make most pleasant walking, helped by grazing keeping the grass short. Whilst usually quiet, there may be military activity on Fingringhoe Ranges across the water.

11. The path runs inland of salt marshes for another 1¼ miles, before reaching an area altered by sea wall breaches. Follow the path for a short distance along a short straight channel to a few trees. On emerging from the trees turn right, walking below the sea wall on the inside of the borrowdyke (the channel of water formed when earth was dug out to build the wall). The path shown on maps heading north has been breached and whilst the low sea wall to the left can be walked, it is rough going and requires jumping a ditch.

12. Follow the path between the borrowdyke and edge of fields, reaching East Mersea Road after ¾ mile. Turn right, following the road with care for 250 yards to the junction with Colchester Road.

13. To continue the island circuit turn left onto Colchester Road. Alternatively (depending on tides) it's possible to walk across The Strood and catch a bus opposite Pyefleet House.

14. After ⅓ mile take a footpath on the right, running along the sea wall alongside Strood Channel. The patch of trees across the water is Ray Island.

15. Mersea's busy harbour is reached after 1½ miles. Continue on the road passing boatyards, fishing boats and seafood restaurants, then after ½ mile take a footpath on the right. Either cross a boardwalk and turn left along the beach, or follow a grassy path below the road. This passes St Peter's Well and completes the circuit at Monkey Beach after ¼ mile.

SHORT ROUTE

16. Follow 1 – 3 then by a sewage outfall pipe at the end of the beach huts take a path inland which soon becomes a paved lane. After ¾ mile go straight over at a crossroads into Dawes Lane, which soon runs across countryside, meeting East Mersea Road after 0.6 miles.
To the right is a Roman burial barrow, which dates from 100-120AD and was excavated in 1912. Inside a small chamber of Roman bricks was found a lead casket containing a green glass urn in which were cremated remains.

17. Turn left along the road, walking with care for 0.4 miles to the junction just before The Strood, then follow instructions from 13.
There is no sea wall path between Mersea and Salcott, so the link to Walk 17 is mostly by road. Two short walks are however possible from the mainland side of The Strood. To the east a footpath runs on a low sea wall, mostly inland of salt marsh, returning to Colchester Road after 1½ miles. To the west is a path across salt marshes to Ray Island. Access is restricted to Essex Wildlife Trust members and permitted only between 1st September & 28th February. (www.essex.wt.org.uk).

WALK 17

TOLLESBURY – SALCOTT CIRCULAR
8 / 4 MILES

A figure of eight, passing through the picturesque villages of Tollesbury and Salcott, along the sea wall and across countryside. Each loop can be followed as separate 4 mile walks if preferred.

Start – Old Hall Marshes RSPB Reserve (Alternative starts at Tollesbury Village Square (bus)(6), Tollesbury Woodrolfe Green (4) or Salcott village (11))
RSPB Reserve car park - open 9am – 5pm (or dusk if sooner). This is accessed through a gate at the end of Old Hall Lane, which is off Chapel Road from Tolleshunt D'Arcy. Do not park on the lane and take care passing Old Hall Farm.

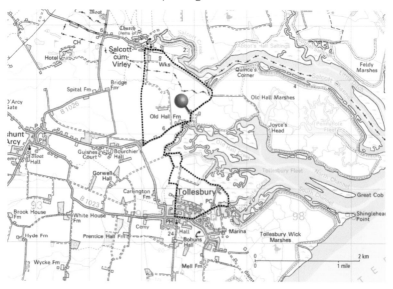

Shops: None on route. Nearest are Tollesbury
Refreshments: None on route. Nearest are Tollesbury
Public Toilets: None on route. Nearest are Tollesbury

1. Take the path from the car park at the opposite end to the entrance, then after a few yards turn right along a grassy path which runs alongside fields, bearing left after a while.

2. On reaching a hard track continue straight on to the sea wall. Turn right along the embankment which is followed for the next 6 miles as you complete a circuit of this ancient marsh.

Mentioned in the Domesday Book, Old Hall Marshes were once owned by Adeliza, sister of William the Conqueror. 16th century sea walls reclaimed the land for farming, although much of it still lies below spring tide heights. In 1984 the RSPB purchased the extensive grazing marshes and two off-shore islands, forming a 1560 acre reserve which is managed as a working farm. Sheep and cattle help achieve different sward heights to suit the huge variety of birds, including 4,000 over-wintering dark bellied brent geese, 2% of the world population.

3. Looking across Salcott Channel you soon get a fine view of a man-made breach in the sea wall, part of managed retreat at Abbotts Hall.

4. If following the shorter walk, after ½ mile take a grassy track on the right. This runs across the marsh alongside pools and channels and reaches the opposite sea wall after ¾ mile. Complete the walk from 8.

5. The longer walk continues on the sea wall, passing Sunken Island towards the end of Salcott Channel.

According to legend this was the site of a gruesome discovery when Salcott villagers came across a drifting customs boat. All 22 men on board were lying dead with their throats cut from ear to ear. It is said that they were buried in the churchyard, with the upturned hull of their boat covering the graves.

6. Approaching the head of the peninsula there are fine views across the water to Mersea, Cobmarsh & Packing Shed Islands, the last of these named after the wooden oyster processing shed

which has been restored by a local Trust. Looking back across the marsh note the thousands of ant hills, formed over centuries by yellow meadow ants.

7.   Quarters Spit at the head of the marsh is reached after 3½ miles. This wild spot has an (inaccessible) shingle beach where terns breed. From here the sea wall bends right, heading along the Blackwater then into Tollesbury Fleet.

8.   After 2 miles the path meets the shorter route, from which a right turn is taken onto the sea wall. Tollesbury and its lightship can be seen across a huge expanse of salt marsh.

Across the channel are lines of fascines; wooden breakwaters constructed with twigs woven between the vertical supports to slow erosion. Other wooden structures are the remains of jetties, once used by the many smugglers who took advantage of the sheltered inlets of the Blackwater and that the nearest customs house was some miles away in Maldon.

9.   The sea wall is followed until ~200 yards before a red-brick house (Ship Ahoy), where steps lead to a grassy path which runs the few yards back to the car park.

WALK 19

TOLLESBURY WICK CIRCULAR
5½ MILES

A walk along the remote northern bank of the River Blackwater, starting at the isolated village of Tollesbury and passing through a marshland nature reserve.

Start – Tollesbury Village Square (bus) or Woodrolfe Green Car Park

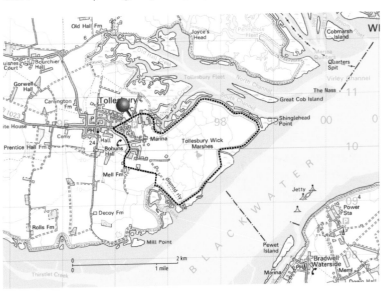

Parking: Tollesbury village centre, Woodrolfe Green Car Park
Train: Nearest are Kelvedon or Witham, then bus
Bus: Tollesbury (limited)
Shops: Tollesbury
Refreshments: Pubs (food?) & café at Tollesbury
Public Toilets: Tollesbury Woodrolfe Green Car Park

1. If starting from the village square head down High Street, which soon becomes East Street and when this divides after ¼ mile bear left into Woodrolfe Road. The car park is on the left after ¼ mile.

2. Continue straight on (or turn left from the car park), then after ¼ mile take a raised path on the right opposite Tollesbury Yacht Club.

Ahead are Tollesbury's famous sail lofts, which were built at the turn of the 20th century to serve the local fishing fleet and later used as stores for wintering J class yachts. These fast and elegant racing yachts, which were owned by wealthy Edwardians, have a long association with Tollesbury and took part in the America's Cup challenge.

3. The path runs above an open air swimming pool then in front of The Harbour View, clubhouse of Tollesbury Cruising Club. An intriguing sign states that the pool's capacity is 1000 people and not to enter if you doing so would exceed this. At the end of the small car park take the higher of two paths on the bank above the marina.

4. Just beyond a small mound with a seat on top pass through a gate into Tollesbury Wick Nature Reserve, a 600 acre grazing marsh managed by Essex Wildlife Trust. The path continues along the sea wall which is followed for the next 3 miles.

Moored in one of the many channels amongst the salt marshes of Tollesbury Fleet is a lightship, which surrounded by salt marsh, appears from many angles to be in the middle of land. Built at Dartmouth in

1954, she served in the Tyne Estuary and Bristol Channel. In 1988 she was purchased by the Christian charity, Fellowship Afloat, and renamed Trinity. She is now used as a centre for relaxation, adventure and exploring the environment.

5. As the path bends right a view opens up to Old Hall Marshes opposite, then Great Cob Island. The main Blackwater is reached at Shinglehead Point, a cockleshell bank which is overlooked by a pill box and provides an excellent breeding ground for terns.

6. Continue along the river bank on an exposed stretch of coastline, with Bradwell Power Station directly opposite.

7. After rounding an inlet of salt marsh and completing another ¾ mile back by the river, the remains of a jetty are reached just before Mill Creek.

This is Tollesbury Pier, which once extended almost 600 yards into the Blackwater. Built in 1907, until 1921 this was served by the 'Crab & Winkle' railway which ran from Kelvedon. The pier was constructed with plans to make Tollesbury a Continental port, but these were curtailed by the Great War, although it is still hard to imagine the trains and the steamers to Clacton which ran from this remote spot. The pier's decking was removed in 1940 as a precaution against Germans landing here.

8. The path turns sharp right down Mill Creek. At the bottom of the creek take a path on the right which leaves the river and heads back towards Tollesbury.

9. Follow the path inland between hedges and over a stile, then turn left on reaching a track. This can be muddy. Continue past Wick Farm after which the track narrows to a path. This soon meets a lane which is followed to the village from Mell Farm.

10. Stay on Mell Road for ½ mile. If returning to the car park, as the road bends left becoming East Street, turn right into Woodrolfe Road and continue for ¼ mile. If returning to the village (or making a diversion to explore the village centre) continue along East Street which leads to the Square after ¼ mile.

A longer linear walk to Goldhanger (10 miles) or a 15 mile loop can be made by continuing straight on at 8 and joining Walk 20 at 4.

WALK 20

TOLLESBURY – GOLDHANGER & CIRCULAR
8 / 13 MILES

A walk along the quiet banks of the Blackwater to the historic village of Goldhanger, with the option to return across fields to Tollesbury

Start – Tollesbury Village Square (bus) or Woodrolfe Green Car Park

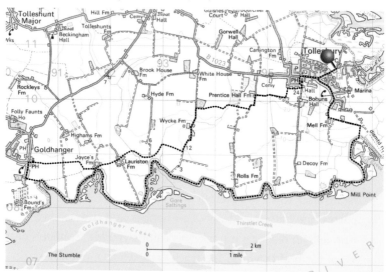

Parking: Tollesbury village centre, Woodrolfe Green Car Park, Goldhanger (considerate street parking)

Train: Nearest are Kelvedon or Witham, then bus

Bus: Tollesbury, Goldhanger (limited)

Shops: Tollesbury

Refreshments: Pub at Tollesbury (no food?) & Goldhanger. Cafés at Tollesbury

Public Toilets: Tollesbury Woodrolfe Green Car Park

WALK 20

1. If starting from Tollesbury village centre, turn right out of the square and head down East Street, staying on the road as it bends right after ¼ mile, becoming Mell Road. If starting from Woodrolfe Green Car Park, turn right up Woodrolfe Road, then left down Mell Road after ¼ mile.

2. After ½ mile a gate is reached at the end of the Mell Road. Take a footpath on the left, continuing on a track straight ahead at Wick Farm after 300 yards. Bradwell Power Station can be seen ahead across the water and close by on the left is a watchtower.

The six-sided, brick-built tower was constructed in 1940 and stands by the former route of the railway line to Tollesbury Pier. It was a Naval Watchtower used as a control centre for mines in the River Blackwater and held radar equipment monitoring the entrance to the estuary.

3. At the end of a tall hedge, ¼ mile from the Wick Farm, turn right, crossing a stile to a path running 250 yards to the sea wall.

4. Turn right along the sea wall, which is followed for 6½ miles to Goldhanger. The winding path by the river and its creeks, passes salt marshes, little beaches and mysterious remains of old jetties, along some of the most remote coastline in Essex.

5. After a while a good view opens up to Osea Island. When surrounded by sea it's hard to believe this can be walked to at low tide. After 2½ miles Rolls Farm is reached and a path inland here could be used as a short route back to Tollesbury.

Right of the farmhouse are the remains of a red hill, one of a number on this stretch of coast. Dating as far back as Iron Age or Roman times, they were formed during salt extraction when seawater was evaporated from pots by burning charcoal. The red colour is due to the effect of firing on the clay soil and broken pots.

6. After a further mile a seat in memory of Nick Felsted provides an ideal spot to rest and enjoy the view towards Gore Saltings, an area of salt marsh that forms islands at high tide.

Just before the next headland is Gore Decoy Pond, which was dug in the 17th century to attract migrating ducks and used until the mid 19th century.

7. An isolated boathouse is passed before heading down the next

creek towards Joyce's Farm. Note that there is no access inland by the farmhouse, so a shortcut to the return route (50 yards away) isn't possible here.

8. The next inlet leads to Goldhanger village, which is set back from the water. At the head of Goldhanger Creek descend from the sea wall and take a path running through a tunnel of hedges, reaching Fish Street after 350 yards.

9. Turn right heading into the village, reaching the centre at The Chequers Inn and St Peter's Church after ¼ mile.

The main road from Maldon towards Mersea used to pass through Goldhanger and travellers would have made use of the 500-year-old Chequers Inn, maybe changing horses at its stables. St Peter's Church dates from the 11th century and includes Roman bricks in its stonework. A pump in the village by the bus shelter was built in 1921 and restored to mark 60 years of Queen Elizabeth's reign.

10. If returning to Goldhanger, walk through the churchyard and continue straight on along a footpath to the right of a hedge. Cross a track after 0.4 miles and continue ahead on a grassy strip between fields.

11. After ¼ mile cross a footbridge at a gap in the hedge and head for the far right corner of the next field (the path across this narrow field may not be clear and it can be easier to go straight across then turn right at the hedge).

12. Pass through a gap and turn left, walking on the right side of a hedge until reaching a gate after 175 yards. Go through the gate and proceed alongside a paddock, passing right of Joyce's Farm.

13. At the end of the paddock turn left, then right on reaching a low barn. Follow the path, passing to the right of the barn, sharp left, then after 40 yards, right across a field.

14. Cross a footbridge at the end of the field and continue straight on along a path then roadway, passing to the left of a bungalow. Turn right on soon reaching a lane, then left after 60 yards, passing between barns and to the right of Lauriston Farm House.

Lauriston Farm is managed using biodynamic organic techniques, with rare breed cattle and sheep. 85% of its 225 acres is designated as a Site of Special Scientific Interest.

15. Go through a kissing gate then on exiting a gate at the far end of the field follow the path as it bends right, left, then right, around bushes, then runs to the right of a hedge.

16. Stay on the path as it crosses a track then bends right at the end of the field, soon reaching a footbridge. Cross the bridge and turn left, then after 50 yards, right, along a grassy strip between fields.

17. Turn left after ¼ mile on reaching a paved track and follow this as it passes Wycke Farm. After a further ¼ mile take a path on the right immediately before a wood.

18. After 650 yards, at the corner of the field cross a footbridge then turn left. Cross another footbridge after 125 yards and continue straight on to the right of the hedge, then straight across the next field.

19. On reaching a tarmac lane ¼ mile from the second bridge, turn left. After ¼ mile take a path on the right opposite two houses.

20. Take the left fork where the path splits after ⅓ mile (right is private). After 200 yards go left into a sports field. Walk across or around the field towards the war memorial and exit, then left, reaching Tollesbury Square after a few yards. To return to Woodrolfe Green Car Park at the end of the square turn right down East Street.

A long walk along the bank of the Blackwater can be made by staying on the sea wall at 8, then following sections of Walks 21 & 22 to Maldon.

WALK 21

HEYBRIDGE - GOLDHANGER CIRCULAR
8 / 6 MILES

A circular walk across country to the picturesque village of Goldhanger, returning along the bank of the Blackwater. If preferred the walk can be shortened by two miles, missing Heybridge Basin and starting from Goldhanger but there is more limited parking here, especially on summer weekends.

Start – Daisy Meadow Car Park Heybridge Basin

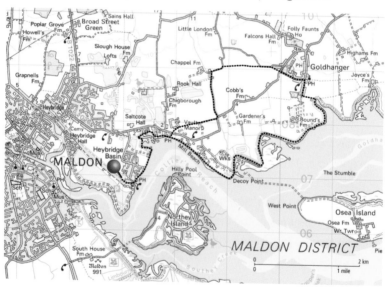

Parking: Daisy Meadow Car Park Heybridge Basin
Train: Nearest are Hatfield Peverell or Witham, then bus
Bus: Heybridge (regular), Goldhanger (limited)
Shops: None on route

Refreshments: Pubs & cafés at Heybridge Basin, pubs at Goldhanger.
Public Toilets: None (removed by Council in 2010)

1. Climb steps from the end of the car park and turn left along the canal towpath, reaching the sea lock after 300 yards.

The Chelmer and Blackwater Canal enters the sea through a sea lock at the picturesque Heybridge Basin, where cargoes were transferred to barges for transporting inland. The attractive row of cottages were badly damaged in WW2 after British traitor Lord Haw Haw wrongly told the Germans that Heybridge was a submarine base. Two historic pubs, The Old Ship and The Jolly Sailor (built 1798) stand close to the lock.

2. Turn left along the sea wall, which is followed around Collier's Reach where coal was once unloaded and the site of Essex Salt Works which closed in 1839, then past Blackwater Sailing Club and Heybridge Mill House. The mill itself was demolished after floods in 1953.

3. Just after six fishing shacks which stand over the water, you pass the slipway to Millbeach Marine Club then The Mill Beach pub. Turn left immediately after the pub and proceed to the road.

4. Take a footpath directly opposite, which is negotiated through a caravan park. First head diagonally right across a small grassy area, heading for a gap in the far corner (100 yards). Follow the path as it bends right, then continue straight on, crossing a roadway to pass through another gap after a short distance. Cross another roadway then leave the caravan park through a gap in the far corner of a small grassy area.

5. Continue straight on along a grassy path between fields, which passes through a gap just beyond a farm building then runs to the right of a hedge.

6. Turn left on the road then immediately left onto the quiet Wash Lane, which is followed for ~1 mile. Soon after Thatched Cottage the lane bends right and after a further 300 yards, on a sharp left bend take a footpath on the right.

7. Follow the path which crosses fields in a straight line with a view ahead to Goldhanger Church, until reaching a lane.

8. Turn right along the lane then take a footpath on the right after 250 yards, just before the first house. The path runs along the left edge of a field, reaching a road after 225 yards.

9. Cross the road and continue along Head Street, soon reaching the centre of Goldhanger.

This attractive village has a long history of fishing. Some of the many pieces of wood standing in the mud in Goldhanger Creek are likely to be the remains of fish traps from medieval times, or jetties used by 18th & 19th century smacks. In the days before refrigeration catches were kept in fish pits by the river, with corks on the end of strings tied to their tails so they could be located when required.

10. Turn right by the Chequers Inn, down Fish Street, an attractive quiet lane where new and old properties blend well and many of the houses have fishes on their front doors. Just before the end of the road take a footpath on the left, which runs to the left of a playing field and reaches the sea wall after 350 yards.

11. Turn right along the sea wall which is followed for 4½ miles back to Heybridge Basin. At the end of the smaller of two bays the start of Osea Island causeway is reached. It is passable for two hours either side of high tide.

Osea Island was occupied by the Romans and recorded in the Domesday Book as having a well-stocked fishery and enough pasture for 60 sheep. In 1903 a remarkable institution was set up on the island, when shocked

*after seeing a drunken man punch his wife, Nicholas Charrington sold
his brewing shares and built a 'Home for Inebriates'. Sadly the venture
failed, with Osea's isolation insufficient to keep alcohol off the island.
A similar, albeit more upmarket venture, The Causeway Retreat, closed
in 2010 after breaches of care standards in its rehab and detox clinic.
Osea remains private with access sadly permitted only to those using its
luxury holiday accommodation.*

12. Continuing up the estuary, you are now opposite Northey Island,
    the Blackwater's other tidal island. Sir Norman Angell's unusual
    house can be seen across the water.

13. Just beyond Osea Leisure Park, a caravan park with café, are ten
    new chalets, standing on galvanised steel stilts. Modelled on the
    luxury oceanfront beach huts found in the Maldives, at high tide
    they sit just eight inches above the water.

14. The Mill Beach pub is soon reached and if following the
    shorter circular walk turn right here and take directions back
    to Goldhanger from 4. For Heybridge Basin follow the outward
    route along the sea wall, reaching the canal after a mile.

    The walk could be extended to Maldon following Walk 22.

WALK 22

HEYBRIDGE BASIN - MALDON CIRCULAR
4 / 7 MILES

A varied walk along the Blackwater, returning along the tidal River Chelmer and the Chelmer & Blackwater Canal, and passing Beeleigh Falls, a little known Essex beauty spot. A shorter option follows the sea wall and returns along the canal, but misses the River Chelmer.

Start – Daisy Meadow Car Park Heybridge Basin

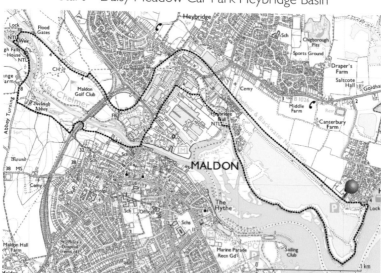

Parking: Daisy Meadow Car Park Heybridge Basin, Maldon
Train: Nearest are Hatfield Peverell or Witham, then bus
Bus: Heybridge, Maldon
Shops: Heybridge, Maldon
Refreshments: Pubs & cafes at Heybridge Basin & Maldon
Public Toilets: Maldon (off route)

1. Climb steps from the end of the car park and turn left along the canal towpath. After 300 yards cross the lock gate by The Old Ship.

2. Turn right onto the sea wall which is followed for the next 2 miles. To the right are water filled gravel pits and to the left Northey Island. The path soon bends right, opening up a view to Maldon.

3. At the end of Heybridge Creek (opposite new houses and Stebbends Way) turn left along a path. After 75 yards take another path right, which runs between reed beds and an industrial area.

4. On reaching a road after ¼ mile leave the path and turn left, then immediately right, meeting a main road after 300 yards. Turn left and follow this for ½ mile.

5. Continue straight on at two roundabouts and cross the bridge over the River Chelmer. To visit Maldon town centre continue up the hill, otherwise turn right along a path above the river bank immediately after the bridge.

6. The path soon heads inland. Turn right on reaching a lane, then just before this bends right continue straight on over a stile onto a path running above the river. This can be very muddy.

7. On reaching a crossroads take the hard path on the right which loops down to the river and back to pass under the Maldon Bypass. Turn right onto a path leading from the road and follow this under trees to a lane, passing Beeleigh Abbey.

Founded in 1180, much of Beeleigh Abbey was destroyed in the Dissolution in 1536. A Tudor building was added to the surviving chapter house and calefactory, which after use as a farmhouse was restored in the early 20th century and purchased in 1943 by William Foyle of Foyles Bookshops. His grandson Christopher, the present owner, is continuing restoration and opens the gardens to the public on certain days each summer.

8. Turn right on the lane passing Beeleigh Grange Farm and reaching Kingfisher Cottage after 300 yards. Ignore the No Entry sign which doesn't apply to walkers and continue along the track ahead.

9. Just after the lane bends sharp right by a large brick wall, go through a kissing gate on the left, joining a path under trees that soon crosses the Chelmer at Beeleigh Falls.

Beeleigh Falls, a series of locks, falls and weirs that combine to make a most attractive feature, link the River Chelmer with the Chelmer and Blackwater Navigation. Waterfalls are a rarity in Essex but although man-made and a small drop, with footbridges across fast flowing water, Beeleigh Falls are well worth a visit.

10. Immediately after the footbridge turn right, heading downstream for 125 yards until reaching the canal. There is a lock to the left, but turn right on a tarmac path which soon crosses a second weir.

11. With Beeleigh Lock and an attractive red-brick bridge on your left, continue along the right bank of the canal. Maldon Golf Club is to your right.

12. After following the canal for ½ mile, cross a bridge (the second after the weir) and turn right, continuing on the left bank, which is followed for a further 2¼ miles. The canal passes fields, houses and industry and under several bridges, before reaching the car park at Heybridge Basin.

SHORTER ROUTE (4 MILES)

Turn right on the main road at 4 and left at the roundabout, then descend to the canal after crossing it on a bridge, following the left bank back to Heybridge Basin.

The longer route could be extended to 11 miles by turning left at 5 and following Walk 23 around Maldon.

WALK 23

MALDON CIRCULAR
4 MILES

A varied walk around the interesting town of Maldon, passing historic wharves, the causeway to Northey Island and the site of the Battle of Maldon, returning across fields.

Start – St Peter's Church (Plume Building), Maldon High Street

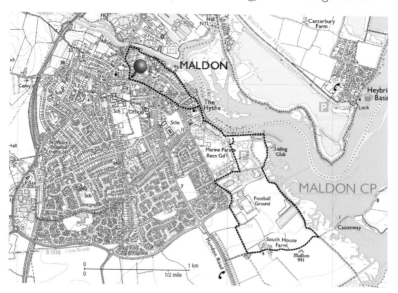

Parking: Car parks in Maldon
Train: Nearest is Chelmsford, then bus
Bus: Maldon (frequent)
Shops: Maldon
Refreshments: Pubs & cafés in Maldon
Public Toilets: Maldon town & Promenade Park

The restored 13th century tower dominating Maldon High Street is all that remains of the medieval St Peter's Church. The nave was replaced with a new building in the 1690s by Thomas Plume, Archdeacon of Rochester, who bequeathed his library of 8,000 volumes to the town. The ground floor, which was originally a school, is now the Maeldune Heritage Centre housing the Maldon Embroidery and the first floor containing Plume's books, one of the country's oldest reference libraries.

1. Descend the steep Market Hill and turn right along Fullbridge Quay at The Toll House just before the Chelmer Bridge, then follow the road as it bends left becoming Chandlers Quay.

2. Where the road bends uphill continue straight on along a path between fences just above the river. After Bath Place Wharf the path bends slightly inland between houses and black weatherboard buildings, before reaching Downs Road.

3. Turn left along the road, then on reaching a crossroads continue straight on (slightly left), soon reaching The Queen's Head.

You are now at The Hythe, the main area of Maldon's historic port, where boats were built, Thames barges loaded with food for London and fishing vessels set sail into the estuary. Thames barges can still be seen by the quay and operate cruises on the Blackwater and beyond. Adjacent to the quay is the popular Promenade Park.

4. Follow the paved sea wall until reaching a breakwater (at the end of which is a statue of the Saxon warrior Bryhtnoth) just after the boating lake, then turn right crossing a roadway to Maldon Yacht Club and joining a path between trees to the right of a fence.

5. After 80 yards turn left onto a track on the river wall, then just before this ends take a footpath on the left in front of a fence. The path (which can be very muddy) is followed along the sea wall for ½ mile to a kissing gate.

To the left of the gate is the causeway to Northey Island, another Essex tidal island. Owned by the National Trust, Northey may be visited at low tide by prior arrangement with the warden (nationaltrust.org.uk/ northey-island). The island contains a large area of undisturbed salt marsh and grazing meadow which is a high tide retreat for waders and *wildfowl. Its one house was built to unusual design by Sir Norman Angell, a writer, politician, member of the Executive Committee of the League of Nations and Nobel Prize winner, who bought Northey in 1923.*

6. Turn right along the lane, passing South House Farm, then right onto a footpath along the edge of the field opposite a cottage (No. 4).

By the sea wall to the left of the lane is Britain's oldest recorded battle site. It was here that the Battle of Maldon took place in AD 991. Viking invaders camped on Northey Island with the important strategic town of Maldon in their sights. As the Saxon defenders led by Earl Bryhtnoth easily held the narrow causeway, Viking leaders asked to be allowed to cross unhindered, in order that a fair fight could ensue on the mainland. In one of the less inspired military decisions of our history, Bryhtnoth agreed to their request only to lose his life in the fierce battle after which the survivors of both sides retreated.

7. At the end of the field the path turns right then left and passes Maldon Town Football Club, before reaching Park Drive. Turn right, passing a leisure centre and reaching the entrance to Promenade Park after ¼ mile.

8. Enter the park and either cut across sports pitches or follow the roadway as it bends left, to return to Hythe Quay. Turn left up Church Street by The Jolly Sailor, passing St Mary's Church with its distinctive white steeple, a beacon for sailors since 1740.

9. Turn right at the top of the road and follow High Street back to St Peter's.

WALK 24

MALDON – MAYLANDSEA & CIRCULAR
8 / 12 MILES

Starting at the busy quay in Maldon, the walk follows quiet Blackwater sea walls with excellent views to Northey and Osea Islands, then down the long Lawling Creek, either ending at Maylandsea or returning across fields to Maldon. Some of the paths on the return route are little used and may not be clear.

Start – Hythe Quay / Promenade Park, Maldon / Finish – Maylandsea village

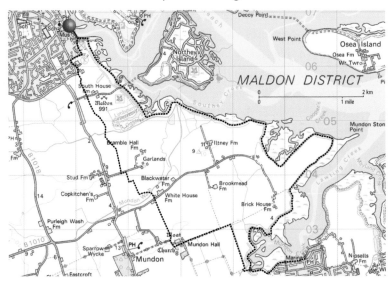

Parking: Promenade Park Maldon, Maylandsea (street)
Train: Nearest is Chelmsford, then bus
Bus: Maldon (frequent), Maylandsea (regular)
Shops: Maldon & Maylandsea

Refreshments: Pubs & cafés in Maldon. Pubs in Maylandsea
Public Toilets: Promenade Park

1. Starting at Hythe Quay or Promenade Park, follow the paved sea
    wall until reaching a breakwater just after the boating lake, then
    turn right crossing a roadway to Maldon Yacht Club and joining a
    path between trees to the right of a fence.
2. After 80 yards turn left onto a track on the river wall, then just
    before this ends take a footpath on the left in front of a fence.
    The path (which can be muddy) is followed along the sea wall for
    ½ mile to a kissing gate.
3. Cross the lane to Northey Island and continue on the sea wall,
    which is followed for 7 miles to Maylandsea (or 6 miles for circular
    walk). To the right is the site of the Battle of Maldon (see Walk 23).
4. Some maps show the path running around Limbourne Creek 600
    yards from Northey causeway, however the creek is dammed
    and a path continues straight on beside Blackwater.
5. The path soon bends right at Mundon Wash Sluice from where
    a former canal heads inland.
*Built in 1832 and just 1¼ miles long, the private canal linked White
House Farm in Mundon with the Blackwater. Although it became disused
as long ago as 1880, the remains of a lock to the sea were only removed
in 1974 when the lower part of the canal was converted to a drain.*
6. After 3 miles by the river, then inland of salt marsh, the path bears
    sharp right down Lawling Creek.
*A narrow path leads along the marshy promontory to Mundon Stone
Point, but whilst this can be negotiated with care part way along the spit,
it's not possible to reach the point. Enjoy the good view to Osea Island
and look out for seals which can sometimes been seen on mud banks
in Lawling Creek.*
7. A footpath on the right towards Brick House Farm could be taken
    as a short cut to Mundon Hall on the return route, but otherwise
    continue along Lawling Creek, which becomes Mundon Creek.
8. For Maylandsea stay on the sea wall for a further ¾ mile to the
    marina, then take the road on the right for shops and bus. For the

circular route to Maldon turn right at the head of the creek on meeting St Peter's Way, a 41 mile route from Chipping Ongar to Peter-on-the-Wall chapel at Bradwell.

9. After 150 yards cross a footbridge on the right and turn left, continuing alongside a drainage channel for 150 yards to another bridge. Turn right here, crossing the field towards a post (the path may not be clear).

10. At the end of the field turn right walking along a grassy strip to the right of a ditch. Cross a footbridge after ¼ mile and carry on straight over the next field (the path runs at about 10° angle to the right).

11. Cross another footbridge after ¼ mile and head towards a post straight across the field. Turn right at the end of the field.

12. On reaching a field with scattered ancient oak trees stay to the left (by the ditch), then after a short distance take a path on the left between bushes. Continue on the left hand side of a pond (the moat of Mundon Hall) for a further 80 yards, then take a path on the left heading to St Mary's Church.

A most attractive building with a timber framed tower and 16th century porch, St Mary's is now in the care of Friends of Friendless Churches who have carried out a great deal of work to preserve and restore the building. Visitors are welcome to look inside although there is no electric light. An annual service is held.

13. Walk through the churchyard and continue on the lane soon meeting the driveway to Mundon Hall. Where the lane turns sharp left after 175 yards take a footpath on the right which bends to the left of a hedge after 50 yards.

14. At the end of the field follow the path between bushes then bear left as it runs to the right of a tall hedge, meeting New Hall Lane after 300 yards. Turn left on the lane, then right onto a path after 25 yards.

15. After 200 yards cross a concrete bridge over Mundon Wash, then head diagonally left following the path for 150 yards through some young woodland. Turn right on emerging from the wood, continuing along the right edge of the field.

16. At the end of the field turn left, staying by the hedge (path may not be clear here), then after 150 yards go through a gap into the next field. Turn left again and after 50 yards right across the field towards a post (track may be unclear).

17. Turn left by the hedge at the edge of the field just before reaching a farm track, then right over a footbridge onto the track after 100 yards.

18. Cross the track and take a path opposite which runs in a straight line across a large field, heading towards a large white house with red tiled roof. Turn right at the end of the field, then left over a concrete bridge after 175 yards.

19. Turn left from the bridge, then after 125 yards head right, crossing the field towards a footbridge (there is no sign and may be no path).

20. Continue straight on at the end of the field towards a white cottage, then pass through a gap in fir trees to reach a lane. Turn right on the lane then left onto a footpath after 20 yards.

21. At the end of the field the path turns right then left and passes Maldon Town Football Club, before reaching Park Drive. Turn right, passing a leisure centre and reaching the entrance to Promenade Park after ¼ mile. Either cut across sports pitches or follow the roadway as it bends left, to return to Hythe Quay.

WALK 25

MAYLANDSEA - ST LAWRENCE & MAYLANDSEA / STEEPLE CIRCULARS
8½ MILES, MAYLANDSEA CIRCULAR 4½ / 10 MILES, STEEPLE CIRCULAR 4½ MILES

Typical Essex coast walks along Blackwater creeks, with good views particularly when the tide is high and the sun shining. There are three options for circular walks using sections of St Peter's Way, two from Maylandsea and one Steeple.

Start – Maylandsea Post Office / Finish – The Stone, St Lawrence
The Steeple circular starts from the Sun and Anchor on The Street.
Start at iii)

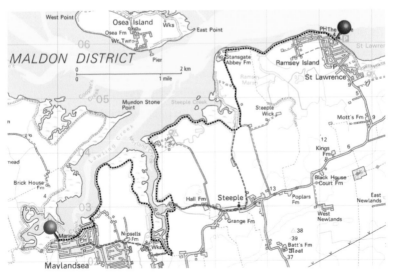

Parking: Maylandsea (street), St Lawrence Bay (car park), Steeple (street)

Train: Nearest is Southminster, then bus
Bus: Maylandsea, Steeple, St Lawrence Bay (limited)
Shops: Maylandsea, St Lawrence Bay
Refreshments: Pubs at Maylandsea, Steeple & St Lawrence Bay
Public Toilets: None

1. Set out down Marine Parade towards the sea. Cross Esplanade and join a short raised concrete path opposite the pub, from which steps on the right lead into a boatyard.

2. Proceed with care through the boatyard for 30 yards, then take steps on the left to the sea wall.

3. Turn right on the embankment passing Maylandsea Bay and Harlow Blackwater Sailing Clubs. The hard path becomes grassy as it takes you up Lawling Creek then turns right around the headland.

4. Follow the path as it bends around salt marsh then sharp right down Mayland Creek, soon dropping down from the overgrown river wall to run along the edge of the marsh for ¼ mile.

5. Rejoin the wall as it turns sharp left, pass three freshwater lakes, then cross a stile as the path heads right towards the foot of the creek.

At the end of the creek the path runs between may bushes, (a spectacular sight with white blossom in spring) passing the remains of Pigeon Dock. Once served by Thames barges, this derelict wooden jetty adds atmosphere to a quiet and picturesque spot.

6. At the head of Mayland Creek the path is joined by St Peter's Way. This is where the circular walk returns to Maylandsea, following instructions from A). If continuing to St Lawrence or taking the longer circuit through Steeple stay on the river wall, following instructions from 7.

A. Take a path on the right 50 yards before the head of the creek. Several paths run through the woods but select the one that runs dead straight through a tunnel of trees. This is St Peter's Way.

B. On reaching Mill Road turn right by Fels Farm, then left along a path where the lane ends by a sewage works. This path can be muddy.

C. Cross a stile and continue across a field heading just to the left of a farmhouse, where another stile leads to a path that runs under trees until reaching a lane.

D. Cross the lane and take the path opposite which runs behind garden fences to Imperial Avenue. Turn right along the road, passing Hardy's pub and reaching the Post Office after ¼ mile.

7. The path stays on the bank as it heads back to the main Blackwater. (Ignore St Peter's Way leaving to the right after ~½ mile.) Steeple Bay Holiday Park is passed at the top of the creek.

8. As the path bends right Osea Island Manor House and pier are clearly seen across the water. Another right bend after ½ mile takes you round the largely salt marsh filled Steeple Creek.

The salt marshes of Steeple Creek are often grazed by sheep. The marsh covering of samphire, sorrel, sea lavender and thrift gives the meat a distinctive flavour and tender texture, such that salt marsh lamb is an increasingly sought-after delicacy.

9. At the head of the creek the longer circular walk returns to Maylandsea via Steeple, following instructions from i). If continuing to St Lawrence stay on the river wall, following instructions from 10.

i. For the longer circular route via Steeple turn right immediately after a gate at the head of the creek, cross a footbridge then a stile.

ii.   Follow the footpath along the right edge of the field, then cross a stile and continue along a grassy path to the right of a pond. After ⅓ mile negotiate a stile and gate then go straight ahead across the next field.

iii. A further gate leads to a path between trees which emerges onto the main road by the Sun & Anchor. Turn right along the road (there is a pavement) for ⅓ mile, passing the Sun & Anchor and St Lawrence and All Saints Church.

iv.   When the road bends left take the lane on the right, signed 'Steeple Bay Caravan Park'. After 350 yards, as the lane bends right, continue straight on through a gate into Steeplehall Farm, passing between the farm buildings and house.

v.   At the end of the farmyard a path (St Peter's Way) continues straight on into a field to the left of a fence. Follow this for 650 yards to the sea wall.

vi.   To complete the Steeple circuit turn right and follow the sea wall for 1½ miles, then pick up instructions from i).

vii. To return to Maylandsea turn left along the sea wall for ~½ mile, then follow the route from A) just after rounding the head of the creek.

10. There is no official path along the next mile of coast and a barbed wire topped gate is soon reached on the sea wall. At low tide it's possible to walk around gate and continue on the sea wall, then drop down to the beach on reaching Stansgate Abbey Farm, but note that it is a steep drop and the beach often slippery.

11. To follow the official route stay on the path which turns right away from the sea wall 30 yards before the barbed wire gate, soon reaching another gate where the path appears to split.

12. Take the path on the left (it may be a bit overgrown) then after 25 yards turn left between bushes. The path comes out on Stansgate Road (marked as a track on the OS map). Turn left along the road which ends at Stansgate and Marconi Sailing Club (not marked on OS map).

Located at a strategic point on the Blackwater Estuary, Stansgate was an important position in both World Wars. Relics of this are the Launching Hard, now used by the yacht club, and the gun emplacement on which the club's race box now stands. In the 19th century Watch Vessel No. 21 was permanently moored here and used by the Coastguard to supervise all craft using the river.

13. A further mile along the sea wall takes you past horse paddocks to Ramsey Island.

Once a true island, a series of land reclamations which started in the 10th century and included blocking up Ramsey Creek, mean that Ramsey Island is now a landlocked part of St Lawrence. It has an attractive, if somewhat exclusive waterfront, with wooden chalets looking out to sea from Scarlett's Estate and Tinnocks Private Estate centred on an attractive (but private) green.

14. Continue along the sea wall until reaching The Stone pub from where a road runs inland through the village. Buses stop close to The Stone and the car park is ~½ mile on the right.

WALK 26

ST LAWRENCE BAY – BRADWELL WATERSIDE
4½ MILES

A short linear walk along a little-known section of the Blackwater. Much of the path sees few walkers and can be fairly rough walking. This walk could be done as an 'out and back' with a break for refreshment at the Green Man, or with an extra mile into Bradwell-on-Sea, a bus can be taken back to the start.

Start – St Lawrence Bay (known locally as Stone) / Finish – Bradwell-on-Sea

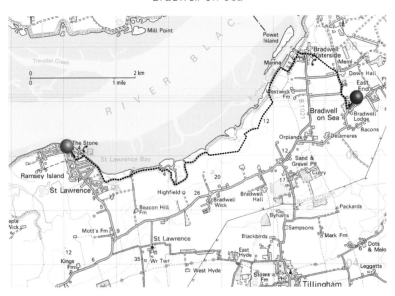

Parking: St Lawrence Bay (car park), Bradwell-on-Sea & Waterside (limited)
Train: Nearest is Southminster then bus

Bus: St Lawrence Bay, Bradwell-on-Sea (limited)
Shops: St Lawrence Bay, Bradwell-on-Sea
Refreshments: Pubs at St Lawrence Bay, Bradwell-on-Sea
Public Toilets: None

The footpath marked on some maps running south east along the river
bank from Stone does not exist, so it is necessary to go slightly inland for
a short distance.
The car park shown on some maps close to the river is not public.
Roadside parking is severely restricted in summer and the public car
park is at Jubilee Fields, ½ mile inland on Main Road.

1. A) If starting at The Stone Inn by the river, head inland along
    Main Road and take the second road on the left, Seaway. As the
    road bends right continue straight on across a few yards of grass,
    onto the river wall.

1. B) If starting from Jubilee Fields Car Park, head down Main Road
    towards the river and after ~200 yards turn right into Moorhen
    Avenue. Just before the last house go through a wooden gate
    in a fence on the right, leading to a short path to the river wall.

2. Turn right along the river wall, passing a caravan site, then bearing
    left as it runs between an artificial lake and Beacon Hill Leisure
    Park. The path soon returns to the river's edge before heading
    inland around the salt marshes of St Lawrence Creek.

3. Shortly after rounding the creek you reach a small wooden jetty
    and slipway. Beyond here the sea wall is impassable, having been
    breached in several places, an excellent example of managed
    retreat.

4. Climb a stile and follow the path for a mile between fields and
    the newly formed salt marsh.

The sea was allowed through the wall in the 1990s but skeletons of
trees still stand, marking former field boundaries. An attractive water
meadow is formed where the highest areas flood at high tide.

5. Soon after returning to the riverside, where Pewet Island can be
    seen just off shore, the path reaches Bradwell Marina.

Pewet Island is a narrow strip of shingle and salt marsh which provides shelter for boats using the marina and roosts for a variety of birds. North west of the island is a wooden fish-weir dating from Saxon times.

6. On reaching the marina turn right, follow the path along the bank, then walk through the boatyard, passing the clubhouse. Turn left by the observation tower.

7. Do not walk as far as the river but take a path on the right ~30 yards from the tower. After a short distance this comes out on Waterside Road. The river is close by on the left and the Green Man ~75 yards to the right.

Dating from the 16ᵗʰ century, with oak beams and whitewashed ceilings, the Green Man is an unspoilt freehouse, offering food, drink and accommodation. Once the haunt of smugglers, much of its custom now comes from yachtsmen, ramblers and bird watchers.

8. To continue the walk into Bradwell-on-Sea village head up Waterside Road for ~175 yards and where the road bends sharp right take a footpath on the left. This crosses fields and comes out at the junction of Trusses Road and High Street. Cross the road and continue ahead along High Street to the village centre.

A longer circular walk could be made continuing on the sea wall at 7 and joining Walk 27.

WALK 27

BRADWELL-ON-SEA – PETER-ON-THE-WALL CIRCULAR
6 MILES

A lovely coastal walk passing cockleshell beaches, open sea and England's oldest church, returning on a quiet Roman road to the village of Bradwell-on-Sea. The circular walk is best started from Bradwell village for parking and buses. Alternatively just the coastal section can easily be done as an out and back walk in reverse from Peter-on-the-Wall, maybe with a break for lunch at the Green Man.

Start - Bradwell-on-Sea village

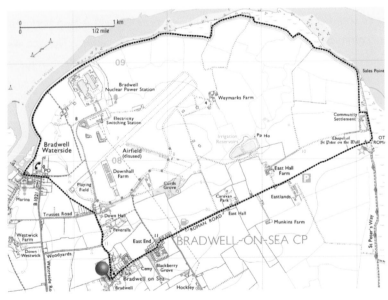

Parking: Bradwell-on-Sea, St Peter-on-the-Wall (½ mile)
Train: Nearest is Southminster, then bus

Bus: Bradwell-on-Sea (limited)
Shops: Bradwell-on-Sea
Refreshments: Pub Bradwell-on-Sea, café on Roman Road
Public Toilets: None

1. Leave St Thomas' Church in the centre of Bradwell-on-Sea, walking down High Street, with the King's Head on your left.
2. On reaching a T-junction with Trusses Road follow a footpath diagonally opposite. The path runs alongside garden fences, crosses two fields and ends in a short alleyway, coming out by The Old Post Office.
3. Follow the road to the right, reaching the Green Man after ~100 yards. This small settlement where the road ends at a slipway is Bradwell Waterside.
4. Opposite Bradwell Quay Yacht Club turn right onto a footpath running along the grass covered sea wall. The now closed Bradwell Nuclear Power Station is soon passed.

The UK's second commercial Magnox power station, Bradwell opened in 1962 and ceased generating in 2002. It is undergoing a long period of decommissioning, a process that will take a whole century. The site will not be cleared and ready for re-use until 2104. The government wants to build a new nuclear plant at Bradwell, once more disturbing the peace of the Essex coast.

5. Beyond the power station is a beautiful, almost white shell beach, which stretches for more than a mile as the Blackwater Estuary ends and the North Sea begins. It's worth a slight diversion to walk on the shells or the grass between beach and salt marsh. Across the estuary are the beach huts of West Mersea.

6. At Sales Point you are alongside open sea. The path turns to the right and with no salt marsh for natural protection, the sea wall is concrete covered.

This is a spot that looks entirely different at low and high tide. At high water the sea laps up to a sandy beach, with no indication of the expanse of mud to be revealed as the water falls. Eleven gravel-filled barges can be seen sitting on the mud, grounded here to help reduce erosion. Lines of wooden stakes in the mud are fish traps dating from Saxon times.

7. To the right of the path you soon pass a patch of woodland in which are the buildings of the Othona Community, formed in 1946 as a place to explore peace and reconciliation. Although an ecumenical Christian community, people of all faiths, or of none, are welcome to stay.

8. In an opening beyond the trees is the chapel of St Peter-on-the-Wall, the oldest church in England.

In AD653, at the invitation of King Sigbert of the East Saxons, St Cedd arrived in Essex from Lindisfarne and founded a Christian community. Using stone from a ruined Roman fort, he constructed a chapel based on the style of churches in Syria and Egypt. It was built on the site of the fort's gatehouse, the wall of the fort – hence Peter-on-the-Wall. The chapel remained in regular use until the 14th century, when with the population having moved inland, it fell into disuse, eventually becoming a barn. After being handed back to the Diocese in 1920, restored and rededicated, it became a place of pilgrimage and worship.

9. Turn right by the church and follow a track heading inland for ½ mile until it meets a lane at a parking area. Follow the lane ahead, a Roman Road, into the village of Bradwell-on-Sea.

To the right of the road is the site of RAF Bradwell Bay, a frontline WW2 airbase. Night-fighter squadrons were based here, equipped first with the Douglas Havoc, then the de Havilland Mosquito. Being close to the coast, many aircraft in distress landed here. 121 members of allied air forces 'left this airfield to fly into the blue forever'. Several hangars are used for storage by farmers and the control tower is a private house.

10. On entering the village the road passes a small school before reaching St Thomas' Church and completing your circuit.

The walk can be linked with Walk 28 by continuing on the sea wall at St Peter-on-the-Wall.

WALK 28

BRADWELL-ON-SEA – BURNHAM-ON-CROUCH
15 MILES

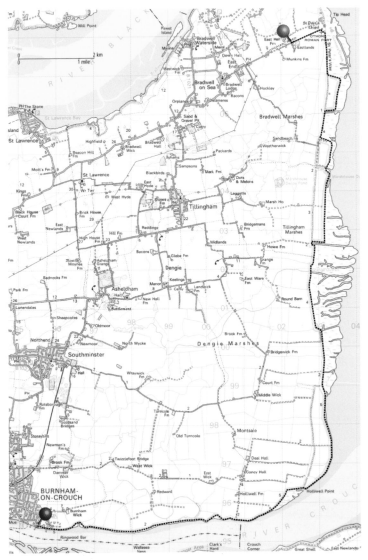

A remote sea wall walk beside salt marshes, open sea and the River Crouch. This is possibly England's most remote coastline and is the longest distance with no settlements on the whole of the country's coast. With few walkers the paths can get overgrown, especially in mid-summer. There are very limited options to cut the walk short, so it is essential to wear suitable clothing and carry adequate food and drink. Treat this like a remote moorland walk. It is one of Britain's great coastal walks.

Start - St Peter-on-the-Wall, Bradwell/ Finish – Burnham-on-Crouch Quay

Parking: St Peter-on-the-Wall (by Eastlands at end of Roman Road)
Train: Burnham-on-Crouch (regular)
Bus: Bradwell-on-Sea (limited), Burnham-on-Crouch (regular)
Refreshments: Pub Bradwell-on-Sea, pubs & cafés Burnham-on-Crouch
Public Toilets: Burnham-on-Crouch

The length of this walk means that either a lift or taxi to the start may be necessary. Alternatively use the infrequent bus to Bradwell-on-Sea village and walk 1½ miles along Roman Road to St Peter-on-the-Wall car park.

1. From the car park proceed straight ahead along the path to St Peter-on-the-Wall chapel.
St Cedd's chapel, the oldest church in England, is usually open to visitors.

Holy Communion is celebrated weekly and an annual pilgrimage takes place on the first Saturday in July.

2. Turn right in front of a small wood and follow the path onto the sea wall. Turn right and follow the sea wall for 14½ miles of wonderful remote Essex coast.

3. After ¾ mile turn left onto the outer sea wall. The wall bends inland again after a further ¾ mile where Glebe Outfall enters the sea, a lovely spot when the tide is high.

4. The inner wall is rejoined after ¼ mile. The path divides after a further 0.4 miles at Sandbeach Outfall. St Peter's Way continues straight on for a short distance then heads inland, eventually to Ongar. It can be used as part of a circular route back to Bradwell, passing Glebe Farm. Otherwise turn left, following the embankment back to the sea. To the left is a line of transmitters for an early warning defence detection system.

5. Marshhouse Pumping Station is passed, then after a further 1¼ miles the path turns inland by the remains of a wooden bird observatory. Turning left after ¼ mile at Howe Outfall, the sea wall runs inland of a huge expanse of salt marsh. The red-brick Bridgewick Pumping Station is passed after 1½ miles.

Built in 1949 by Essex Rivers Control Board, this is one of a number of outfalls that drain the marshes inland of the sea wall, allowing their use for agriculture. They are welcome features for walkers, breaking up the long sea wall sections. Looking back, on a clear day Peter-on-the-Wall is still just visible across the marshes.

6. After Coate Outfall is passed (1 mile) you are back by the sea
    (or mud according to tide), walking on the concrete Deal Hall
    Wall above cockle shell banks. A gate across the wall has for
    many years been adorned with assorted items removed from
    the beach, a reminder of how mankind is polluting our oceans.

7. The path gradually bends right, reaching Holliwell Point at the
    mouth of the River Crouch. Concrete pillboxes overlook a small
    beach. The next 5½ miles follow the river bank into Burnham. A
    mine watching tower is passed after 1 mile, the largest of many
    WW2 defences in this area.

8. As the River Roach is passed on the far bank, Foulness Island
    with its mysterious military installations gives way to Wallasea, an
    island returning to nature. Entering Burnham-on-Crouch, pass a
    boatyard then the Royal Corinthian Yacht Club.

*The grandest of Burnham's four sailing clubs, the Royal Corinthian was
originally founded on the Thames in 1832. Its distinctive white clubhouse
was built beside the Crouch in 1931. As 'Corinthians' the members are
strictly amateur and no professional seamen or paid hands are allowed.*

9. Follow the paved walkway along the waterfront then turn right
    to the main street by the Anchor Hotel. For the station (¾ mile)
    turn left.

WALK 29

BURNHAM-ON-CROUCH – ALTHORNE –
NORTH FAMBRIDGE
5½ / 10½ MILES

An easy riverside walk, with good views, birdlife, yachting interest and options of two finishing points, both with regular trains returning to Burnham. If preferred the walk can easily be done in reverse, enabling refreshments to be enjoyed in Burnham before catching a train back to the starting point.

Start – Burnham-on-Crouch station or Quay / Finish – Althorne or North Fambridge stations

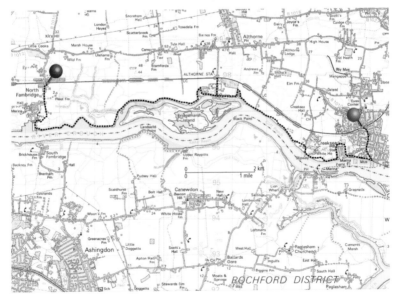

Parking: Burnham-on-Crouch, Althorne, North Fambridge
Train: Burnham-on-Crouch, Althorne, North Fambridge (regular)

Bus: Burnham-on-Crouch, Althorne, North Fambridge (limited)
Shops: Burnham-on-Crouch
Refreshments: Pubs at Burnham-on-Crouch, North Fambridge, cafés at Burnham-on-Crouch
Public Toilets: Burnham-on-Crouch

1. Turn right out of Burnham-on-Crouch station, following the road for ¾ mile to the town centre, or from car parks head to quay / town centre.
2. By the war memorial, which is beside the river where several houseboats are moored, turn right, following a red-brick path that runs along the quay.
3. Pass two of Burnham's four yacht clubs, then some large houseboats and Riverside Park. Veer right, following the path as it runs around the large basin of Burnham Yacht Harbour. Make your way with care between the Swallowtail bar and large yachts, regaining the path to the right of the RNLI station.
4. Continue on the path as it rejoins the main river, until it meets Ferry Road which takes you around a small inlet, home to Creeksea Sailing Club.

Creeksea is reputed to be the place where King Canute attempted to hold back the tide (a claim also made by Bosham in Sussex). Creeksea Place, a large Tudor mansion, was reputedly a home to Anne Boleyn.

5. A few yards after the creek, as the road bends right, go through a gate on the left adjacent to the driveway to 'Tideways', a rather

nice house but with grounds that bar public access to 300 yards of riverbank.

6. Follow the path along the edge of the field, then pass through another gate, from where steps lead up to the river wall. This is followed for most of the remainder of the walk.

7. After ~1 mile the path goes through a gate, ahead of which is an Essex rarity – a small cliff. Follow the path through a gap in the hedge by an old jetty and ascend the low hill. From this rare elevated viewpoint there are excellent views down the river where the main Crouch runs to the left of Bridgemarsh Island, which is separated from the mainland by Althorne Creek. The high-rise buildings of Southend can be seen poking over the hill to the left. At low tide it's possible to explore the beach and cliff below, where small fossils can sometimes be found.

8. Beachcombers may wish to stop at an attractive shell beach in a little bay about 100 yards beyond the cliff. Just after the start of Bridgemarsh Island the path runs around a small inlet, soon after which it reaches Bridgemarsh Marina, passing on a grassy bank between boats and caravans.

It seems hard to believe that the low lying Bridgemarsh Island, now interspersed with little creeks, was once inhabited. There used to be a brickworks using its deposits of clay and a tramway to take product to a quay, where it was loaded onto Thames barges. The last extraction was after the Great Flood of 1953, when clay was used to fill sea wall breaches on the banks of the Crouch, after which the island was abandoned to wildlife.

9. If heading for Althorne turn right along an unadopted road (private but with right of way for walkers), reaching Althorne

station after ⅓ mile. For North Fambridge continue along the river wall.

10. The path passes a chalet park before rounding a small inlet and continuing along Bridgemarsh Creek. A chimney standing on the island is from the old brickworks. Canewdon Church stands on the hill across the river, a beacon for many miles of coastal walking.

11. A gate marks the start of Blue House Farm Nature Reserve.

This 600 acre working farm is owned by Essex Wildlife Trust and in winter attracts huge numbers of wildfowl and wading birds. Around 2,000 brent geese feed on the fields which have been grassland for the last 100 years. A wide variety of breeding birds can be seen in summer, including barn owls, skylarks and reed buntings. Careful management of the creeks and ditches allows water voles to thrive.

12. As Bridgemarsh Island ends you are once again on the bank of the main River Crouch, which is followed for a further 1½ miles to North Fambridge Yacht Club. About halfway a seat cut from a huge tree trunk provides a fine spot to rest and enjoy the view back down the river.

13. Turn right along the bank just beyond the yacht club, soon reaching the Ferry Boat Inn. This 500-year-old pub was once at the water's edge but sea defences and the changing river bed have left it 200 yards inland.

14. From here the simplest route is to follow the road to the station, possibly with a short diversion (left at Church Road) to see the village's diminutive Holy Trinity Church with its tiny wooden tower, but some road walking can be avoided by taking the footpath which runs through trees to the right of the Ferry Boat.

15. After passing alongside the pub's garden, this soon meets a track. Turn right here, pass to the left of a house and over a stile. Keep to the right of a hedge after ~50 yards and walk along the edge of a field.

16. Cross a footbridge then turn immediately left, following a path which takes you to the left side of a barn and onto a lane. Turn left onto the lane and continue straight on as it reaches the road. North Fambridge station is on the right after ⅓ mile.

WALK 30

NORTH FAMBRIDGE - SOUTH WOODHAM FERRERS
7 MILES

A varied walk across farmland, along an old railway track, the banks of winding creeks and a section of the River Crouch. The route goes some distance from the river but avoids dangerous walking along the busy B1010.

Start – North Fambridge station / Finish – South Woodham Ferrers station

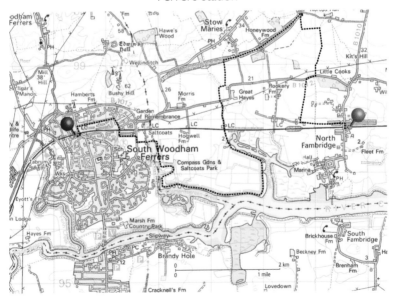

Parking: North Fambridge & South Woodham Ferrers stations
Train: North Fambridge, South Woodham Ferrers (regular)
Bus: North Fambridge, South Woodham Ferrers (regular)

Shops: South Woodham Ferrers
Refreshments: Pubs North Fambridge, South Woodham Ferrers
(both off route)
Public Toilets: None on route. Closest are South Woodham Ferrers
town

1. Turn right along the road from the station. After ~75 yards turn
    left into a residential road, continuing on a track where the road
    ends.
2. On reaching a footpath after 0.4 miles turn right, soon passing
    white farm buildings (Willow View). Don't turn right on the farm
    track but continue straight on the footpath which runs by the
    edge of the field.
3. Cross a footbridge into a tunnel of bushes, then the next field,
    coming out on the B1010 road by bend signs. Turn right, walking
    35 yards on the grass verge, then cross the road, joining a
    footpath opposite. The path runs slightly uphill to the left of the
    hedge, continues across the next field, then by another hedge as
    it climbs towards the summit.
4. Turn left at a footpath crossroads by an oak tree just before the
    top of the hill. The path runs across the hillside and is a good place
    to stop and enjoy the views over the Crouch valley. Canewdon
    Church is to the left, South Woodham Ferrers to the right and
    high-rise buildings of Southend in the distance.
5. A short distance after starting to descend the path meets
    another. Turn right along this path which soon reaches a road.
    Just before the road go down a slope on the left which runs
    between trees, taking you to an old railway line which is followed
    for 1¼ miles.

*The South Woodham Ferrers to Maldon line has been closed to
passengers since WW2, when heavy usage and lack of maintenance had
left it in a poor state. The railway's opening day was marred by tragedy
when a young farm labourer called Arthur Burton was taking a wagon
laden with peas across the new line. As he did so the 3.12 train from
Maldon driven by George Kenzie approached. The fireman sounded his*

whistle but Arthur didn't hurry and the cart was struck. He was taken
by train to Cold Norton station but pronounced dead there by Dr Price.

6. Cross a lane after ¾ mile then return to the track which soon
    passes under a bridge into Stow Marries Nature Reserve.

The 5½ acre reserve includes the remains of the platform which served
the village and nearby WWI airfield, plus an area of meadowland. Four
species of fern; wall-rue, maidenhair spleenwort, black spleenwort and
hart's-tongue, grow in the mortar of the bridge.

7. Leave the railway ¼ mile from the bridge, turning left by a sign
    Stow Marries Halt, onto a path which crosses a footbridge and
    stile before running by a hedge then across a field.

8. On reaching a garden almost at the road turn right, walking to
    the right of a fence to the corner of the field. From here the path
    takes you 300 yards to the road.

9. Cross the road and continue straight over along Little Hayes
    Chase, passing the farm and reaching a railway crossing. Cross
    with care and continue along a track which reaches the sea wall
    by a derelict barn.

10. Bear left onto the sea wall and continue straight ahead following
    the path on the embankment for the next 3 miles. Initially you

are walking along Stow Creek, passing West Wick Marina, before bending right along the Crouch, then down Clementsgreen Creek.

Like many Essex creeks, before the days of the railways and good roads Clementsgreen was used by vessels carrying cargo around the coast. There are records of a jetty here as long ago as 1519 and more recently the creek was used by boats serving a brick and tile works which operated from 1896 to 1910.

11. Pass a dam at the end of the creek, staying on the right bank of salt marsh and a lagoon that were formed when the creek was blocked. At the end of the lagoon turn left towards a sports pavilion and follow the road out of Saltcoats Park. Turn right on the main road, then after 60 yards left into a quiet industrial road.

12. At the end of the road turn right onto a footpath which runs under the railway and to King Edward's Road. Turn left along the road, then after ½ mile left into Hullbridge Road. The station is 150 yards on the right.

The walk can be extended to 13 miles with a riverside circuit around South Woodham Ferrers, by staying on the embankment at 11 and joining Walk 31.

WALK 31

SOUTH WOODHAM FERRERS CIRCULAR
6 – 7½ MILES

A circular walk following the River Crouch and its creeks that surround three sides of South Woodham Ferrers. Although always close to the town, there is less than a mile of (quiet) road walking and the scenery is surprisingly rural. Two options for short cuts reduce the length if preferred.

Start – South Woodham Ferrers station

Parking: South Woodham Ferrers station, Saltcoats Park (start walk from 4), or end of Hullbridge Road (start from 9)
Train: South Woodham Ferrers (regular)
Bus: South Woodham Ferrers (regular)
Shops: South Woodham Ferrers (off route)

Refreshments: Pubs South Woodham Ferrers. Café at Marsh Farm (just off route)
Public Toilets: None on route. Closest are South Woodham Ferrers town

South Woodham Ferrers was no more than a couple of farms until the coming of the railway in 1889, the station acting as junction for the Maldon branch and serving the small village of Woodham Ferrers a mile away. 'Plotland' developments bought people from London to the Essex countryside, where many built bungalows, weekend cottages and smallholdings. Extensive development in the 1960s & 70s formed a 'New Riverside Country Town', although the town seems to have rather turned its back on the water.

1. Turn left from main station car park entrance along Hullbridge Road, then right after 150 yards into King Edward's Road.

2. After ½ mile as the road bends left, turn right into a cul-de-sac King Edward's Road 'Even Numbers', leading to a paved footpath after 75 yards.

3. After passing under a railway bridge take the 2nd path on the left, which leads to a quiet road. At the end of the road turn right onto a main road.

4. After 60 yards cross the road and enter Saltcoats Park. Walk through the car park, left of the pavilion, then take a path immediately on the right at the start of a field.

5. Turn right onto the embankment and follow the path past two lakes. These were once part of Clementsgreen Creek before it was dammed, shortening it by half a mile. On reaching the dam continue on the right bank of the creek, passing the remains of docks and several wrecks.

6. The route continues along the winding creek bank, although there are two opportunities for short cuts. The first takes a track on the right ⅓ mile from the dam and allows a short cut to Marsh Farm, saving ~1½ miles but missing the best riverside walking. The second is after a further ¼ mile where a path runs right as the creek bends left. This reaches the Crouch after ~250 yards and saves almost a mile, but misses the most remote and quietest section of the route.

7. It's worth stopping a while to enjoy the views down the Crouch before bending to the right and heading up the river, whose bank is followed for the next two miles.

8. The walk takes you around Marsh Farm Country Park, an

outstanding grazing marsh, surrounded on three sides by water and winter home to many species of ducks and waders.

9. Just after South Woodham Yacht Club you reach the end of Hullbridge Road, where a diversion of ⅓ mile can be made to Marsh Farm café.

10. The OS map shows a footpath across the river to Hullbridge and whilst this is said to be wadeable at low tide, it's not recommended. There was a bridge here in Roman times, from which the town gained its name and another which was built in the 13th century, but apparently disappeared in the 17th. A ferry ran until 1960.

11. After ¼ mile the path bends right along Fenn Creek, continuing along the bank until diverting slightly inland around Eyott Sailing Club. Should you wish to make a circuit of Eyotts Faron, a small peninsular where the river makes a sharp turn, follow a path to the right of the sailing club. Continuing on the main route turn right onto the road, then left after a few yards taking a path between Eyotts Farm and houses.

12. Follow the path along the bank of the creek, which soon becomes a narrow stream, then cross a stone footbridge leading to Woodham Fen Nature Reserve.

13. The path runs through the reserve to a railway crossing. Cross with care, then after a few yards take a path over a footbridge on the right. Follow the grassy path for 220 yards then turn right under a railway bridge.

14. Continue along a path, a short length of unmetalled road, then a final section of path behind gardens, leading to the station car park.

An 11 mile walk to Battlesbridge can be made by taking the path around the pond at 11 linking with Walk 32 at 3.

WALK 32

SOUTH WOODHAM FERRERS – BATTLESBRIDGE
4 MILES

A short walk along footpaths to the River Crouch and the village of Battlesbridge, where many antique shops may be explored.

Start – South Woodham Ferrers station / Finish – Battlesbridge station

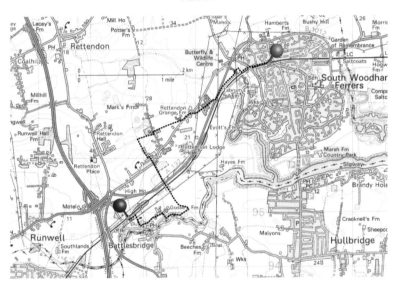

Parking: South Woodham Ferrers & Battlesbridge stations (charged),
Train: South Woodham Ferrers, Battlesbridge (regular)
Bus: South Woodham Ferrers, Battlesbridge (regular)
Shops: South Woodham Ferrers (off route), Battlesbridge
Refreshments: Pubs & cafés Battlesbridge
Public Toilets: None on route. Closest are South Woodham Ferrers town

1. Cross the station car park and turn left along a path running between garden fences and the railway. A short section becomes gravel road before the path resumes.

2. After passing under the road enter Woodham Fen Nature Reserve, taking the left fork parallel with the railway.

The 20 acre Woodham Fen reserve includes a rare transitional area between salt marsh and rough grassland. A wide range of salt marsh plants and wild flowers can be seen, along with birds, butterflies, common lizards and slow worms.

3. On reaching a crossroads by a pond take a smaller path straight on which bends around the pond. A footbridge can be seen across the pond. Opposite a seat take a narrow path on the left which leads to the footbridge.

4. Cross the footbridge and turn left, following the (little used) path along the edge of the field. After ~¼ mile cross a track, staying by the railway until reaching the main A132.

5. Cross this busy road with great care and take the lane opposite, which soon becomes car free. On reaching a road after ⅓ mile turn left.

6. After 300 yards take a path on the right next to a garden centre entrance. This bends left and comes out in a field. Continue along the edge of the field by the tall garden centre hedge, passing through a gap at the end and emerging behind kennels.

7. The path continues by the hedge, crossing two stiles, then after passing greenhouses comes out on a narrow lane. Turn left on the lane then right after a few yards through a gate which is set back ~40 yards from the road.

8. Follow a pleasant path running through a tunnel of trees until reaching a crossroads of paths from where there are excellent views across the Essex countryside and to the distant Kent hills.

9. Turn left on the path to the left of a large oak tree, following a grassy path downhill and into a wood. Here it can be overgrown but is worth it for the mass of wildflowers that may be seen.

10. On reaching a road take the path directly opposite. This starts wide and grassy but soon narrows. You may need to climb a gate at the end.

11. Carefully cross the A132 once more and go straight on over a railway bridge onto a track which runs downhill towards the narrow but still tidal Crouch. Just before the river (0.4 miles) take a narrow path along the hedge to the right, which soon drops down to the river bank, passing a large barge. The distinctive shape of Battlesbridge granary can be seen ahead.

12. The path ends at a lane which is followed left for ⅓ mile into the picturesque village of Battlesbridge. You may wish to spend a while exploring antiques shops and enjoying refreshment.

A small port in medieval times, by the 19th century Battlesbridge was a thriving community of mills, farms, coal yards, lime kilns and maltings. Small fishing boats plied the river, catching smelt, whiting, flatfish and the occasional salmon. The traditional riverside industries and goods transport were in decline by WWI and in 1932 a fire destroyed one of the remaining mills. Since the 1960s Battlesbridge has been reinvented as a popular centre for antiques, with many properties on the north side of the river used for the sale of antiques and collectables.

13. To reach the station take a path on the right of the lane just before the village green. This runs between fences and meets an unmetalled road after ~¼ mile. Turn left along the road, soon reaching the station.

There is no access to the south bank of the Crouch from Battlesbridge, so to link with Walk 33 it is necessary to continue along the road.

WALK 33

HULLBRIDGE WALKS
3½ MILES (EAST), 3½ MILES (WEST)

Two short walks along the banks of the River Crouch from Hullbridge. There are pleasant walks along the river in both directions from Hullbridge but the section is isolated by a length of private river bank towards Battlesbridge and a breach in the wall beyond Brandy Hole. The walk could be continued to Battlesbridge but with ¾ miles along a fairly busy road with no pavement.

Start – Poole's Lane Car Park, Hullbridge

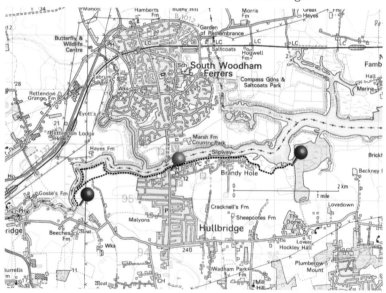

Parking: Hullbridge

Train: Nearest is Hockley, then bus or walk

Bus: Hullbridge (regular)

Shops: Hullbridge
Refreshments: Pubs / restaurants at Hullbridge. Pubs & cafés at
Battlesbridge
Public Toilets: Hullbridge (car park)

HULLBRIDGE WEST

1. From Poole's Lane Car Park turn right down Ferry Road and
    almost immediately go through a gate opposite the entrance
    to The Anchor (pub/restaurant), entering the woods and grassy
    glades of Kendal Park.

*The 9 acre Kendal Park Nature Reserve includes the only natural
woodland on the River Crouch, some of which is coppiced to produce
different ages of tree growth. The varying levels of light, warmth and
shelter, along with a recently established pond, encourage a wide range
of plants and animals.*

2. After 300 yards bear right as the path drops down to the river
    bank and carry on to the end of the woods. Continue on the
    roadway between houses and the river, then after 100 yards take
    a narrow path on the right, which reaches the open river wall
    after a further 100 yards.

3. After 0.4 miles, where the river bends right the official footpath
    continues straight on, away from the river. This can be followed
    for ½ mile to make a circular walk, however it is little used and
    may be somewhat overgrown. The easier option is to stay on
    the river wall on a good path as it follows the bend opposite
    Hayes Farm.

4. If following the circular walk ascend steps and turn right where
    the path reaches the river and return along the river wall,
    reaching Hullbridge after 1½ miles.

5. A good point to turn round on the out and back walk is 150
    yards beyond the steps, at a gap in the hedge where the path
    runs inland for a short distance. Turning back here and following
    the river bank to Hullbridge makes a 3½ mile walk.

6. To continue to Battlesbridge go through the gap in the hedge
    and follow the path as it runs along the edge of the field then

back by the river and on to the road, which is reached after ¼ mile. Turn right along the road then right again after almost ¾ mile, soon reaching Battlesbridge.

HULLBRIDGE EAST

1. From Hullbridge Car Park or bus stop walk 100 yards downhill to the slipway, then turn right along the riverside path.

2. The path runs between chalets then expensive houses and the river, looking across to Marsh Farm Country Park. Brandy Hole Yacht Club is reached after 1 mile.

3. Brandy Hole, which adjoins Hullbridge, gained its name from a smuggling reputation. It's thought that tea, rather than liquor was the main contraband that passed through here, enabling many of the locals to become rich.

4. Brandy Hole slipway is reached after a further ¼ mile, from where the path narrows, initially running between bushes, then onto a narrow slither of land between the river and creek.

5. This ¼ mile walk is one of the strangest in Essex, especially at high tide when walking just above the water level one appears to be standing in the middle of the river. It results from a breach in the river wall and the formation of an extensive salt marsh, which is a notable spawning area for a variety of fish.

6. The land stops abruptly and despite the path shown on the OS map, there is no way across the breach. Turn back here, retracing the outward route to Hullbridge.

Breaches in the sea wall mean that to reach South Fambridge it is necessary to head inland onto paths and roads at Brandy Hole.

WALK 34

SOUTH FAMBRIDGE - CANEWDON CIRCULAR
9 / 12 MILES

A walk along the quiet south bank of the Crouch, returning inland through the village of Canewdon. Optional out and back extension towards Brandy Hole (A-C).

Start – South Fambridge

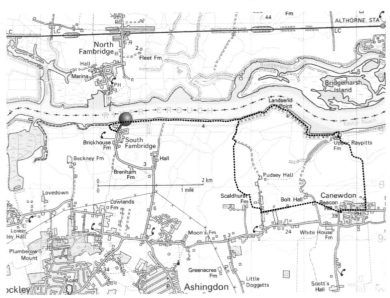

Parking: South Fambridge & Canewdon (street)
Train: Nearest is Hockley, then walk
Bus: Canewdon (limited)
Shops: Canewdon
Refreshments: Pub in Canewdon
Public Toilets: None

Park on gravel at the end of Fambridge Road just before it turns right into St Thomas Road.

1. Follow a track at the end of Fambridge Road, taking the left branch where it splits after a few yards and reaching the sea wall after 300 yards.

South Fambridge, was for many years linked by ferry to North Fambridge across the river but plans to build a bridge in the 1930s came to nothing. The village holds a little known role in our aeronautical history, with the wide, straight, calm waters of the Crouch used in development of the sea plane in the early 1900s.

2. Turn right on the sea wall, which is followed for the next 3 miles. The path bends right after 2 miles at Landsend Point, from where you are now opposite Bridgemarsh Island. A chimney from the old brickworks can be seen still standing on the island.

3. Just beyond a small salt marsh filled bay with old wooden jetties extending into the river, Upper Raypitts Farm is reached. Leave the river wall here, taking a signed path just before a barn.

4. Cross the roadway, go through a gate in the hedge and head diagonally across the field, passing a small derelict stone building. After 100 yards bear left, reaching the entrance to a large field after 100 yards.

5. There is no clear path, but head either across or along the right edge of the field to a gate almost at the far corner. Cross two footbridges and turn right, heading uphill towards Canewdon

along the right edge of a large field. Looking back there are excellent views across the Crouch valley.

6. The path becomes a track, passing houses then reaching Canewdon opposite the village school and shop. Turn right, then continue straight on by The Anchor.

The Anchor is said to be haunted by the ghost of a young woman named Sarah, who had a relationship with a wealthy landowner in the 1500s. When she inevitably became pregnant the man's wife found out and told him to lock her away. This he did in the building that was later to become The Anchor, but after giving birth poor Sarah was cruelly murdered.

7. St Nicholas Church is reached after ¼ mile.

St Nicholas Church is most notable for its massive tower, which commands outstanding views of the Crouch and Thames estuaries. A light used to be maintained here as a guide to shipping. Legend has it that so long as the tower stands there shall be six witches in Canewdon, but if a stone falls from it one will die. Outside the church is the village lock up and stocks, which date from around 1775.

8. Walk through the churchyard and take the right hand path of two opposite, which descends across a field with good views of the river.

9. Cross a farm lane after ¼ mile and follow the path to the left of the hedge, continuing straight on where the hedge turns right.

The path leads to a track (Larkhall Avenue) which is followed to Pudsey Hall Lane.

10. Turn right on the lane, then left over a footbridge onto a path after 125 yards. The path bends right crossing another footbridge after 150 yards, then a further footbridge after ¼ mile.

11. Follow the edge of the field then turn left at the next bridge after 300 yards. Pass through a gap in the hedge after 75 yards and continue on the path as it runs up a gentle slope towards the river.

12. On reaching a track after ½ mile turn left, arriving back at the river bank after ¼ mile. Turn left, retracing your steps back to South Fambridge.

13. The walk may be extended by crossing a stile and continuing westwards along the concrete-topped river wall from South Fambridge. After a mile the path bends left down a creek, which was formed when the sea wall was breached in 1953. The path still shown on the OS map is impassable, crossing 50 yards of water or deep mud.

14. The path bends right after a further ½ mile opposite a track to Beckney Farm which is signed as private to walkers so cannot be used to make a circular route.

15. The hard topping soon ends and although a rough path continues on the river wall, further channels block the route to Brandyhole. This is probably a good point to turn back, making a 3 mile out and back walk from South Fambridge.

Longer walks can be made by staying on the sea wall at 3 and linking with Walk 35.

WALK 35

CANEWDON CIRCULAR
6½ / 8 MILES

*A circular walk from a 'village of witchcraft', across farmland and along
the Crouch, with excellent views to the river and beyond. A slightly longer
option crosses the head of Paglesham Creek. This can also be followed
as a 3 mile circular walk from Lion Creek (A-E).*

Start – The Anchor, Canewdon

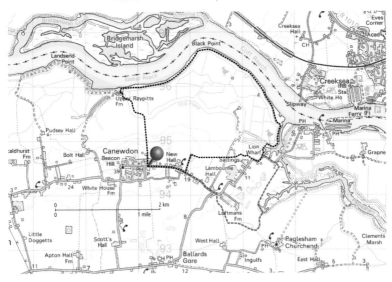

Parking: Canewdon (street)

Train: Nearest is Rochford, then bus

Bus: Canewdon, Loftmans Corner (limited)

Shop: Canewdon

Refreshments: Pub in Canewdon

Public Toilets: None

The pleasant village of Canewdon once had a sinister reputation, with all its residents considered as possible witches and outsiders unwilling to visit. It was believed to be an unlucky place for wheeled transport and wagoners avoided it for fear of having their wagons bewitched.

1. From The Anchor head along High Street, passing two shops, then turn left into Gays Lane opposite the village school.

2. Follow the narrow lane past houses, then descend the hill at the edge of a huge field with excellent views across the Crouch.

3. On reaching a footbridge and gate do not take the vague path directly towards the river, (this reaches barbed wire and a broken footbridge) but although there is no path this way, bear left at a 45° angle across the field heading past a small pond (often dried up in summer) and towards Upper Raypits Farm. (Note that a bull is sometimes kept in this field).

4. Pass through a gap in the corner of the field just past a cattle trough and follow the grassy path for a short distance to a gate (behind a ruined shed).

5. Turn right and follow the farm track in front of a barn, bearing left just before a pond and continuing onto the river wall. You are now opposite Bridgemarsh Island.

6. Turn right onto the river wall, which is followed for the next 2½ miles. The path is paved as far as Black Point, where it bends sharp right. Soon after here you pass opposite The Cliff (see Walk 29.)

The wetland to your right is Lower Raypits Nature Reserve, a complex of saltmarsh, intertidal and grazing habitats that serves as a notable feeding and roosting area for wildfowl and waders. Dykes and seawalls support nationally scarce plants, including beaked tasselweed, sea barley, curved hard-grass and grass vetchling.

7. On reaching Lion Creek the path turns sharp right. This is a good spot to sit and enjoy the views. The cranes across the water are a dock on Wallasea Island, beyond which can be seen the waterfront of Burnham-on-Crouch.

8. Follow the path to the head of Lion Creek, passing a white boathouse on the opposite bank. From here you have three options for returning to Canewdon.

SHORT ROUTE (AND ROAD)

9.   Turn right on reaching Creeksea Ferry Road. From here the simplest way back to Canewdon is 1¾ miles along the lane, turning right at Loftmans Corner (buses stop here), but a shorter route crosses fields (sometimes ploughed with no path).

10. Follow the road as it passes Lion House, bends sharp right then sharp left. At the left bend cross a stile on the right and follow a path between a large garden and horse paddocks.

11. After ~80 yards pass through a kissing gate. The path from here may be unclear but aim diagonally left to the end of a line of trees 40 yards away, then walk along the left edge of the trees.

12. At the end of the trees head slightly left across the field towards a footbridge (posts are just visible). Cross the next (small) field to another footbridge leading to a larger field.

13. Head towards the centre of a small wood diagonally left, or if there is no path turn left and follow the edge of the field, turning right at a ditch at the end of the field. Either way reaches a footbridge in the corner of the field.

14. Cross the footbridge and head diagonally across the field ~60 yards to the near corner of a line of trees which surround an attractive pond.

15. Turn right, walking alongside the trees, then left at the end of the pond onto a wider path that takes you to Lambourne Hall Road. Turn right and follow the road into Canewdon.

LONG ROUTE

A.   Turn left on the road then take a footpath on the right after 350 yards, where the road bears left. The path crosses a small bridge, runs along a low embankment, then between a field and salt marsh. Where you see telegraph wires go straight on underneath them and don't take what appears to be a path on the right. After ⅔ mile turn left at a gap between a hedge and fence, onto the sea wall at the head of Paglesham Creek.

B.   At a gate after 225 yards turn right down steps and follow the path away from the creek, walking to the left of a water channel.

After ¼ mile this becomes paved at a pumping station. 40 yards beyond this turn right across a gap in the channel, then right to the edge of the field which is followed alongside another drainage channel.

C.   Cross a footbridge after 175 yards and turn left along a little used path on the right bank of the channel. This bears right shortly before reaching farm buildings and soon reaches a track.

D.   Turn right on the track then pass through a gap straight ahead when it reaches a hedge. Proceed slightly left across the field in a direction just to the right of a large house. Turn left at the end of the field, then right over a stile into a small field after 160 yards. Cross diagonally to a further (rather high) stile at the end of the field and continue a short distance to the road.

E.   Turn left on the road, then right at the fork at Loftmans Corner onto Lambourne Hall Road into Canewdon. Alternatively if returning to Lion Creek, turn right on reaching the road.

The walk can be extended (13½ miles) to include a loop through Paglesham by staying on the sea wall at B and following Walk 37 from 3.

WALK 36

WALLASEA ISLAND
4 / 5 / 6 MILES

Three walks along the embankments of Wallasea Island alongside salt marsh and the River Crouch, with good views across the island and to Burnham and Foulness. Wallasea is being developed over ten years as a Wild Coast Project by the RSPB. Additional paths and a visitor centre will be opened, and the current car park may be moved. Expect to see a large number and variety of birds, including avocets in spring and summer.

Start – RSPB Car Park, Wallasea Island

Parking: Wallasea Island (RSPB Car Park), Lion Creek (limited)
Train: Nearest is Rochford, then bus
Bus: Canewdon, Loftmans Corner (limited)

Ferry: Burnham-on-Crouch (summer only)
Shops: None
Refreshments: Marina
Public Toilets: None

Other than very occasional high tides, Wallasea Island (the 9th largest English island) is connected to the mainland and until recently was quiet agricultural land that few people visited. Under care of the RSPB a huge conservation and engineering scheme, using spoil brought in by barge from London's Crossrail construction, is now recreating the ancient wetlands, salt marsh, pasture and lagoons that covered most of the Essex coast before man built the sea walls. A ten mile network of footpaths (partly open at the time of publishing) will allow walkers to explore Wallasea's coast and marshes. Details of progress and paths as they open can be seen at rspb.org.uk.

WALK ONE – JUBILEE MARSH TRAIL (5 MILES OUT & BACK)

1. From the car park ascend the sea wall and turn right. After 0.9 miles take a path on the right which crosses the island to Jubilee Marsh.

Jubilee Marsh was so named because it was started in Jubilee year. The viewpoint at the end is called Half Moon Viewpoint as the field in the southeast corner used to be called Half Moon because of its shape.

2. Take the left fork where the embankment divides after 300 yards. On a small mound after a further mile is one of the smaller

tunnel-boring machines that excavated Crossrail, providing earth that has raised the level of Wallasea.

3.   The walk ends after a further ½ mile at Half Moon Viewpoint, a remote spot by the River Roach from where there are views to Foulness and Potton Islands.

4.   Retrace the outward route to return to the car park.

WALK TWO – ALLFLEETS MARSH TRAIL
(4 MILES OUT & BACK)

The trail has been named Allfleets by the RSPB after an old name for some fields on the island. The viewpoint is called School House after the school house that stood about half way along Jubilee Marsh until the 1920s.

1.   From the car park ascend the sea wall and turn right, walking parallel with the Crouch inland of salt marsh that has been formed by breaches in the original sea wall.

2.   School House viewpoint from where there are good views across the island and to Foulness opposite, is reached after 2 miles.

3.   Retrace the outward route to return to the car park.

WALK THREE – LION CREEK (6 MILES OUT & BACK)

1.   From the car park turn left along the sea wall, heading towards the marina and wharf which are reached after 1½ miles. The ferry to Burnham-on-Crouch runs from the marina.

2. After a further ¼ mile the sea wall bends left down Lion Creek. At the head of the creek turn right following the road for 550 yards until a footpath on the right (just after passing a distinctive white boathouse).

3. Follow the path along the embankment for 350 yards, passing between Lion Creek and lagoon, then when it bends sharp right take a path on the left. This runs between bushes and ends at a bird hide after ¼ mile.

The lagoon is part of an Essex Wildlife Trust reserve and was once part of the creek. Cut off by a new sea wall and bounded on three sides by the old one, the lagoon contains brackish water and in late summer has an attractive border of salt marsh plants such as sea lavender, golden samphire and sea spurrey.

4. Retrace the outward route to return to Wallasea car park.

5. From Lion Creek links can be made to Canewdon or Paglesham walks.

WALK 37

PAGLESHAM CIRCULAR (NORTH)
5½ MILES

A circular walk on well-maintained paths, through picturesque Paglesham, across farmland and along the tranquil banks of Paglesham Creek and the River Roach. The walk links the two centres of Paglesham village, Churchend and Eastend.

Start – The Punch Bowl, Paglesham Churchend

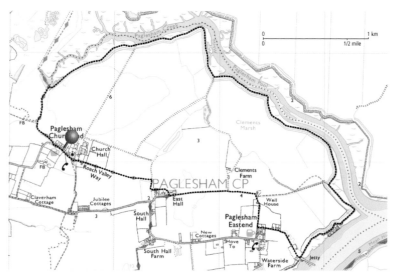

Parking: Roadside parking between St Peter's Church and The Punch Bowl at Paglesham Churchend and limited at Paglesham Eastend.

Train: Nearest is Rochford

Bus: Closest practical bus service is Loftmans Corner or Ballards Gore.

Shops: None
Refreshments: Pubs Paglesham Churchend, Paglesham Eastend
Public Toilets: None

Surrounded by atmospheric creeks and marshes, and with picturesque red-brick and weatherboard houses, Paglesham retains the romantic atmosphere of smuggling for which the village was once famous. More legitimate trade came from its fine oysters which were reared in the creeks and river, and continue to be farmed by traditional methods in the River Roach.

6. Facing The Punch Bowl, head left down the lane, then right after ~50 yards along a concrete footpath.

7. Follow the path as it runs alongside a water channel until reaching salt marshes at the head of Paglesham Creek. Turn right and walk along the sea wall, which is followed for the next 3 miles.

A WW2 pillbox where the embankment bears right on meeting the wider channel provides a good point to look around at the view. Paglesham and Canewdon churches can be seen behind, the boat house at Lion Creek to the left, cranes of Wallasea Island ahead and the yacht clubs of Burnham slightly to the right.

8. The winding sea wall eventually brings you to the River Roach, the only significant tributary river in Essex. Turning right, continue along the bank, passing rusting hulks of boats and disused oyster beds, until reaching a boatyard and pontoon.

9. Turn right, walking through the boatyard and continuing along a lane on the right of the car park.

10. As the lane bends sharp left after ¼ mile take a footpath right that runs by a house, through a gate and comes out on the edge of a field. A short detour would be to continue on the lane for 100 yards to the Plough & Sail.

11. Stay on the path as it takes you through the garden of Well House, coming out at the end of East Hall Lane. Follow this quiet lane for ~½ mile until reaching a pair of barns. A footpath runs around the barns and along the edge of the field.

12. Stay on the path as it bends right at the corner of the field,

then sharp left through a gap in the hedge after 100 yards. The path runs at the edge of another field, then between fences and hedges, before coming out on the lane by St Peter's Church.

Of Norman origin, but built on the site of an earlier Saxon church, St Peter's was restored in 1883 by Zachary Pettit, who had a beautiful stained glass window built in memory of the five of his nine children who died in childhood.

13. Continue a short distance along the lane, passing a line of attractive cottages, until reaching The Punch Bowl.

The walk can be extended to 9½ miles by staying on the sea wall at 5, following Walk 38 but turning left on the road at Walk 38 at 8, then right on the lane, joining Walk 37 at the barn by East Hall.

WALK 38

PAGLESHAM CIRCULAR (SOUTH)
5½ MILES

A circular walk on along the River Roach, returning across countryside to the historic village of Paglesham.

Start – Plough and Sail, Paglesham East End

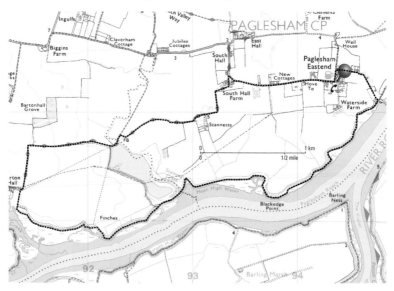

Parking: Paglesham Eastend (limited roadside)

Train: Nearest is Rochford

Bus: Closest practical service is Loftmans Corner or Ballards Gore

Shops: None

Refreshments: Pub Paglesham Eastend

Public Toilets: None

An inn for at least 300 years, the Plough & Sail retains much of its original white weatherboarding. Centre of village activities for centuries, it has been a meeting place for fishermen (30 oyster smacks worked from Paglesham in 1890), a haunt for smugglers and bakehouse (which villagers could use to cook bread or pies on payment of one penny).

1. Follow the unadopted lane to the left of the Plough & Sail, reaching a private car park by the river after ⅔ mile. Keep to the left of the car park, pass through a boatyard and turn right onto the river wall by the jetty which is followed for the next 2¾ miles. (The path on the embankment along this isolated stretch of the River Roach is little used and grass may be long).

2. The river wall bears left soon after a WW2 pillbox marking the entrance to Bartonhall Creek. Continue straight on, turning left after 25 yards along a shell covered track running inside the embankment.

3. On reaching a T junction by farm buildings, turn right along a track which immediately bends left rising gently away from the river.

4. The track bends sharp right towards a lake after ¼ mile. Havengore Bridge to Foulness can be seen on the horizon. After a while the path is shown running between trees then behind a hedge but it's easier to stay on the farm track which takes you to Stannets Creek Lagoon.

The once navigable Stannets Creek has been dammed, forming a lagoon which provides a valuable watering and preening site for resident wildfowl and over-wintering for birds, such as dark- bellied brent geese.

5. Note that signposts and some maps may not match paths that are seen on the ground. Continue straight on for ~100 yards across the end of the lagoon, then take a track bearing left down from the embankment.

6. After 30 yards take a rough track on the right (easily missed) leading to the edge of the field on the right. This soon becomes a narrow path running to the right of a hawthorn hedge.

7. Continue straight on when the path becomes an earth track at a gap in the hedge, then a winding hard track at Stannets, an early

18th century weatherboard house that was once home to the jazz musician Digby Fairweather.

8.   Bear left between barns of South Hall Farm, then right along the road passing Cupola House as you return to the Plough & Sail.

The impressive red-brick Georgian Cupola House is notable for its turret on the roof, which whilst assumed to be innocently ornamental was actually constructed to allow residents to keep an eye on the Government excise men on the creeks.

The walk can be extended to Rochford by turning left on the track at 4 and joining Walk 39 at 9 to regain the sea wall.

WALK 39

ROCHFORD / GREAT STAMBRIDGE CIRCULAR
8 / 5½ MILES

A circular walk across countryside, passing a convenient pub for refreshment and returning along the banks of the Roach. A shorter circuit starts at Great Stambridge (start from 9).

Start – Rochford station or The Royal Oak Great Stambridge

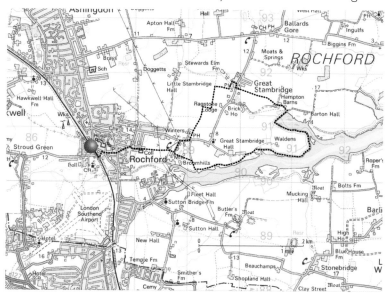

Parking: Rochford station & town, Great Stambridge (limited street)
Train: Rochford (frequent)
Bus: Rochford (frequent), Great Stambridge (limited)
Shops: Rochford
Refreshments: Pubs Rochford & Great Stambridge, cafés Rochford
Public Toilets: Rochford

1. Turn right from Rochford station and car park (adjacent to Southend-bound platform), cross the road and at the roundabout bear left up West Street.

2. Continue straight on past Market Square, cross South Street and immediately bear left at East Street.

With a market charter granted by Henry III in the 13th century when Southend was a mere hamlet, Rochford was the most important town in the area. It retains character with many surviving ancient buildings, narrow streets and alleys.

3. As East Street bends left and becomes Stambridge Road, turn right into Rocheway. When the road ends continue on the footpath across a field.

4. Turn left on reaching a lane. On reaching Stambridge Road after 300 yards turn right, crossing to walk on the pavement. After 250 yards take a footpath on the left immediately after The Cherry Tree pub.

5. Follow the path along the edge of the field, going straight on where it meets another path after 500 yards, then turning right at the junction with a wide path after ~250 yards.

6. After 200 yards take a footpath on the left in front of a hedge, continuing straight on for 300 yards as the path narrows at the end of the hedge.

7. On reaching another hedge turn right following a path between two fences. This ends with a short stretch of lane to the main road. Turn right immediately passing The Royal Oak, where you may wish to stop for refreshment.

8. After ~100 yards cross Ash Tree Court and take a path on the left, which is followed for ¾ mile until reaching a lane just beyond a barn.

9. Turn left along the lane for 250 yards until a sharp left bend, then walk a few yards to the sea wall on the right. This is followed around Bartonhall Creek, reaching the main River Roach after almost a mile.

10. The next 2½ miles follows the sea wall almost to the end of the tidal Roach.

The Roach was once a busy river, with commercial shipping, fishing and of course smugglers. Perhaps the most famous vessel to sail its waters was

HMS Beagle, which carried Charles Darwin on his scientific expedition to the Pacific and spent her final years here as a coastguard ship.

11. As you approach boatyards on the far bank ignore a path on the right, continuing on the embankment for a further 250 yards until the path turns inland. Follow the path past the edge of a cricket field, turning left between trees just before the pavilion.

12. The path passes between two ponds then continues a short distance across a field to a lane. You are now just a few yards from where the outward route emerged at the lane 4.

13. If returning to Great Stambridge turn right, following instructions from 4. If returning to Rochford turn left on the lane and take a footpath on the right after 70 yards.

14. The path soon turns sharp left, then crosses two footbridges by the site of Stambridge Mills, before heading towards Rochford.

Stambridge Mills, a large flour mill, lay derelict for some years after closure in the late 1990s, but at the time of writing was being replaced with luxury flats. Built in the 1850s, the mill processed corn from the Rochford area, flour being taken down the river by barges.

15. Turn right on meeting another path and continue alongside the Roach which is now just a stream, reaching Southend Road after ⅔ mile. Turn right, cross the road and stay on the left, reaching Rochford station after ~½ mile.

There is no access for walkers to the south bank of the Rochford end of the Roach. To link with Walk 40 requires road walking then a footpath past Butler's Farm, joining Walk 40 by Bolts Farm at 7.

WALK 40

LITTLE WAKERING & BARLING CIRCULAR
6½ MILES

A circular walk around Barling, across countryside, along winding creeks and the River Roach.

Start – Little Wakering Road

Parking: Street parking at Little Wakering
Train: Nearest is Southend East, then bus
Bus: Little Wakering (regular)
Shops: None
Refreshments: None on route. Castle Inn near start /end
Public Toilets: None

1. The starting point is on a straight section of Little Wakering Road, opposite the end of Little Wakering Creek and between the village signs for Little Wakering & Barling. Buses stop close by and street parking is possible.

2. 50 yards north of the footpath running from the creek (along which you will return) turn left onto a path running by a stream between houses. (Note that this is not the track to Clump Farm). The footpath soon reaches a field, where it runs to the left through a tunnel of low trees.

3. On reaching a cottage pass through a gate and continue by the fence on the right for ~60 yards, then cross a stile to a lane. Cross the lane and take a footpath almost opposite (slightly to the right). After a short distance this passes through a gate at the end of a paddock, then runs straight across a field.

4. On reaching the hedge at the end of the field turn left along the side of the field, then pass through a gate on the right after ~150 yards.

5. Cross the road and continue on a path in a straight line across a large field, then turn left on reaching a lane, soon passing Barling Magna Nature Reserve.

Once part of Southend's defunct sewage farm, this 12 acre site has been turned from a general dumping ground into a nature reserve by volunteers. Owned and maintained by Barling Magna Parish Council, the reserve includes a newly created wood which was planted by schoolchildren to celebrate the Queen's Diamond Jubilee in 2012.

6. Where the road turns sharp left by Bolts Farm take a grassy footpath on the right, running past Roach Farm and coming out on the Roach opposite Bartonhall Creek.

7. Turn right and follow the sea wall for the rest of the walk. After 2 miles Barling Ness is reached, almost opposite Paglesham Eastend. Here you turn sharp right alongside The Violet as you round Barling Marshes. Opposite is Potton Island.

8. The path soon veers right again, heading down Barlinghall Creek, one of the many waterways around the Essex Archipelago.

Essex has more islands than any other English county, six of them in this archipelago between the rivers Roach & Thames. Seals can sometimes be seen in the channels between the islands.

9. Continue past the quay at Barling, which is partly formed from a WW2 concrete barge (see Walk 50). Barling Hall is to the right and the 12th century All Saints Church a little inland.

The small village of Barling was originally known as Barling Magna, a name retained for the parish which includes Little Wakering. The name is said to derive from the Saxon words 'ban' for boar and 'ing' meaning meadow.

10. Stay on what is now a low sea wall, soon bending right down Little Wakering Creek. Take a paved path at the end of the creek, which brings you to Little Wakering Road after ~100 yards. The Castle Inn is ~⅓ mile to the left.

This walk links directly to Walk 41, giving the possibility of a 15 mile figure of eight route.

WALK 41

LITTLE WAKERING CIRCULAR
8½ MILES

A circular walk around creeks of the Essex Archipelago, a little known cluster of islands between the Crouch and Thames.

Start – Corner of Little Wakering Road & Kimberley Road (just north of The Castle Inn & Little Wakering church)

Parking: Street parking at Little Wakering

Train: Nearest is Southend East, then bus

Bus: Little Wakering (regular)

Shops: None

Refreshments: None on route. Castle Inn near start /end

Public Toilets: None (facilities at Wakering Boatyard are private)

1. Proceed ¼ mile to the end of Kimberley Road and take a footpath on the right, running along the south (right) bank of Little Wakering Creek. The sea wall is followed for the next 5½ miles.

2. After 1½ miles the path bends left at a stile, heading up Fleethead Creek in a long loop around low lying grazing marsh.

The area of salt marsh between the two creeks is known as Brimstone Hill, although it rises no more than a few feet above sea level. Named after the Brinson family who originated from Normandy, there is evidence it was occupied around 1300, possibly with some form of hunting lodge.

3. After passing the quay at Barling the path bends right up Barlinghall Creek. Across the water is the old Barling Marsh tip. Canewdon can be seen in the distance.

4. On reaching the confluence of three channels the path bends right. To the left is The Violet, at the end of which can be seen the River Roach and Paglesham boatyard. You are now following Potton Creek, passing the old crossing point to Potton Island opposite after ¼ mile.

Potton Island has been populated since Neolithic times and was home to several arable farms before catastrophic flooding in 1884 ruined the soil. It wasn't until the 1940s that agriculture was successfully re-established, however the Great Flood of 1953 inundated Potton once more, trapping 11 people who had to be taken off the island by boat, and 450 sheep who were swum to safety. In 1955 Potton was purchased by the MoD and a 'Blast and Fragmentation Range' established.

5. Potton swing bridge is reached after a further ~½ mile. This is

opened on request but only at high tide is there sufficient depth for boats to pass. It is not permitted to cross the bridge. You are now on MoD land and access is only allowed on the mainland sea walls.

6. Wakering Boatyard and some large house boats are passed, before following the path around Mill Creek. The main creek is re-joined opposite the channel between Potton & Rushley Islands. The bridge to Havengore Island and Foulness can be seen ahead.

Accessible only by a low tide ford, Rushley Island is owned by the MoD. Its only building, a barn, stands out on the flat, low lying land. The island is protected by a 3 mile sea wall, which was initially constructed by John Harriott of Great Stambridge, the founder of the Thames River Police, who purchased Rushley for £40 in 1781, with the aim to develop it for agriculture. An exceptional tide in 1791 flooded the island and Harriott had no funds left to effect repairs, so was forced to abandon his project.

7. The ford to Rushley is reached just before the tiny settlement of Oxenham, where the route heads inland. Descend steps and follow the roadway between farm buildings and three houses. As this bends left take a grassy footpath (Footpath 14) on the right, heading away from the barns.

8. Follow the path along the right edge of the field, bearing left to a footbridge after 300 yards. Continue across the next field to another footbridge, then straight on by the left edges of the next two fields.

9. Turn left on reaching a road, then after ¼ mile right along

Footpath 12 just before the road bends left. The footpath is a tarmaced road for 200 yards before becoming a track which divides 75 yards after a farm.

10. Take the left fork and turn right on meeting a path, with glimpses of a lake on the right. Turn left at the end of the lake, soon passing the 15th century Little Wakering Hall.

11. Turn right by the hall entrance, then left after a few yards on a track running to the left of a barn. After 350 yards take a grassy footpath on the left, then cross a stile on the right after 225 yards.

12. Head diagonally left across the field to another stile. (Alternatively turn left alongside the edge of the field to reach the beautiful Norman St Nicholas Church or The Castle Inn).

13. Continue straight on to a stile by an avenue of trees. Cross the private road and enter the field opposite heading for another stile. Cross this and aim for the far left corner of the field and another stile. Turn left, soon reaching Little Wakering Road adjacent to Kimberley Road.

Subject to military activity a link to Walk 42 can be made by staying on the creek wall at 7.

WALK 42

SHOEBURYNESS RANGE CIRCULAR (RESTRICTED ACCESS)
4½ MILES

A circular walk through MoD Shoeburyness, mostly on sea walls of the historic ranges, passing one of the most dangerous footpaths in Britain.

Start – Wakering Stairs (parking) or Landwick Gate, Great Wakering (bus)(start at 5)

Landwick Gate is the checkpoint on the road to Foulness. Wakering Stairs is reached by a road on the right from Landwick Gate. This passes through a barrier which is only raised when the range is open for public access.

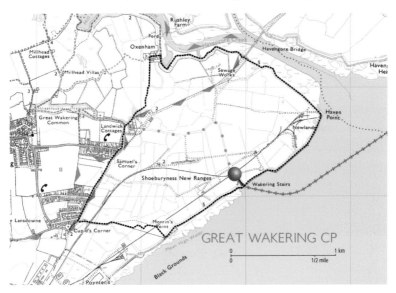

Parking: Wakering Stairs
Train: Nearest is Shoeburyness, then bus or walk

Bus: Landwick Gate & Great Wakering (regular)
Shops: None
Refreshments: None
Public Toilets: None

WARNING: *Most of this walk is on MoD land, part of the Shoeburyness Range. Access is only permitted when red flags are NOT flying, generally (but not always) at weekends and after 5pm. Never pass through closed access barriers or attempt the walk if red flags are flying. The many warning signs must be obeyed. Do not stray from the paths which are marked with red & white poles. Further details can be seen at www. shoeburyness.qinetiq.com.*

The area east of Shoeburyness including Pig's Bay and Foulness Island, known as MoD Shoeburyness, were first used by the military in 1858 when the British School of Gunnery was opened. The extensive tidal sands provide a secure area for long range firing and recovery of shells.

1. From the parking area at Wakering Stairs climb onto the sea wall. Directly ahead is a causeway, the start of The Broomway 'path'.

Running for six miles across Maplin Sands, the ancient low tide route to Foulness has claimed many victims. Although marked on maps, there is no actual track and the tide covers the mudflats faster than a man can walk. The route used to be marked with branches but in disorientating sea mist travellers sometimes still met their death struggling out to sea in rising water. It is strongly recommended not to venture onto The Broomway without a guide. Details of guided walks can be seen at www.wildlifetrips.org.uk.

2. Turn right on the sea wall which is followed for ⅔ mile. Stretching out across the estuary ahead is a gradually decaying defence boom, which was built as a Cold War barrier protecting the Thames and replaced a similar wooden structure from WW2.

3. A fence on the sea wall at Morrin's Point bars access to the next mile of coastline. Turn right along a path which soon crosses one of the disused military railway lines that served the range. Turn left on reaching a field and left again after crossing a footbridge to the next field after 150 yards.

4. Continue on the path at the left of the fields, crossing another railway line and reaching an MoD road after 0.4 miles. Cross the road (it is forbidden to walk along it) and pass through a gate, then turn right at a kissing gate onto a footpath.

5. Follow the path which runs parallel with the MoD road and fence, until reaching a lane after ½ mile. When the lane bears sharp right after 200 yards continue straight on along a track on the left. (If starting from Landwick Gate turn left from the bus stop and right down the track after 150 yards.)

6. Where the track divides after 70 yards take the right option

(Footpath 16), which reaches the settlement of Oxenham after ½ mile. Stay on the track as it bends right beyond farm buildings, reaching the sea wall of Havengore Creek after 125 yards. Opposite is Rushley Island. Turn right along the sea wall reaching Havengore Bridge after ⅔ mile.

Built in 1988, Havengore Bridge replaced an earlier crossing from 1922 that had carried both a road and military tramway to Havengore Island, which is linked to Foulness and New England Islands. The bridge, which has floating pontoons and barriers slung beneath the deck to prevent unauthorised access, can be opened for vessels two hours either side of high tide. Access to Foulness is severely restricted and a pass is required other than for monthly opening of the Heritage centre.

7. After checking that red flags are not flying, follow the footpath under the bridge and pass back into the range. Walkers must stay on the sea wall path which is marked by red and white posts.

8. After ⅔ mile Haven Point is reached. This isolated corner is arguably the mouth of the Thames, as a line from here to Warren Point in Kent is used to calculate the river's 215 mile length. Various military installations here are off the path so must not be explored.

9. Follow the path as it bears right, now following the Thames and reaching Wakering Stairs after ¾ mile.

With public access to the Thames denied by military use, road walking is required to reach Shoeburyness and link with Walk 43.

Walk 43

SHOEBURYNESS – SOUTHEND – LEIGH-ON-SEA
4 / 7½ MILES

Seven miles beside the sea on paved walkways, passing military relics, the world's longest pleasure pier and ending at a quaint fishing village. An easy walk illustrating the variation along Southend's famous sea front.

Start – East Beach, Shoeburyness / Finish – Leigh-on-Sea station

Parking: East Beach, Southend and all along route
Train: Shoeburyness, Southend, Chalkwell & Leigh (frequent)
Bus: Shoeburyness, Southend, Chalkwell & Leigh (frequent)
Shops: Shoeburyness, Southend, Chalkwell & Leigh
Refreshments: Many pubs & cafés on route
Public Toilets: East Beach, Thorpe Bay, Southend, Chalkwell, Leigh

Shoebury East Beach is reached by following a footpath opposite the station (by crossing gate) for ~250 yards.

1. Facing the sea, turn right along a walkway at the end of the beach, which follows the sea wall for ¼ mile before heading inland into The Garrison.

There have been defences at this strategic point at the mouth of the

Thames since the Iron Age. The present day garrison buildings mostly date from the mid-19th century and were Royal Artillery barracks until closure in 1976. With renovation of historic buildings and sympathetic new construction, the site has now been converted to housing.

2.   After 50 yards turn left onto the road alongside Gunners Park. At the end of the road join a paved path which takes you back to the sea wall.

3.   After passing various military relics, turn right across the grass at a coastguard lookout, then left onto a short length of road that takes you back to the promenade, which is followed for the rest of the walk.

4.   At high tide it's an attractive walk through Thorpe Bay to Southend and if the sea has retreated you can expect to see plentiful birdlife on the mud. There is no bay – Thorpe was renamed after its railway station, which was called Thorpe Bay to show it was by the sea. Of interest on the esplanade is a tram shelter, which was built in 1914 and used until the trams stopped running in 1938.

5.   Approaching the busier and louder centre of Southend, the Sea Life Centre then Kursaal are passed. Once the largest fairground in the south of England, this was Southend's main entertainment centre and thousands once packed its 26 acres of rides, amusements, gardens and ballroom.

6.   At Adventure Island, the town's modern fun park, either follow the sea wall around the park and under the pier, or stay by the road. If heading into Southend cross the road and walk up the

hill past The Royal Hotel to the shops and station (extra ½ mile inland).

A possible diversion would be to walk or take the train along the 1.34 mile long pier, the longest pleasure pier in the world. The original and much shorter wooden pier opened in 1830, but was replaced by the current iron structure in 1889, with several extensions and enlargements added later. A series of fires have destroyed most of the buildings but those walking to the end can still enjoy refreshments and view the modern RNLI building.

7. Continuing by the sea the walk soon becomes quieter and after a mile Westcliff is reached. The line of 13 seafront cafés under the arches of Palmeria Parade have been serving food for over 100 years in what were originally fishermen's huts.

8. After a while the path moves away from the road, staying by the sea as it passes a paddling pool and The Crow Stone, which marks the limit of riverbed owned by the Port of London Authority. The current stone has stood here since 1837 and replaced another from 1755 which can be seen in Priory Park.

9. Chalkwell station is passed, its platform backing onto the sea, then a path continues beside the railway to Leigh.

Permanently moored by the bank is HMS Wilton, a former Royal Navy minesweeper, and now home to Essex Yacht Club. She took part in clearing mines from the Suez Canal in 1974 and was the navy's first glass fibre hulled warship, giving her the nickname HMS Tupperware but protection against magnetic mines.

10. Passing Leigh Sailing Club (housed in the old railway station) continue along a cobbled street into the village of Old Leigh.

Unlike the relatively recent development of Southend, there has been a fishing settlement at Leigh for many centuries. It was recorded in the Domesday Book as Legra. A successful port and ship building centre in the Middle Ages, with ships becoming larger and its deep water channel silting up, in the 18th century Leigh reverted to fishing. Boats still bring in shellfish, which are sold from cockle stalls and enjoyed in Leigh's pubs and restaurants.

11. After passing shops, galleries, pubs and a heritage centre, bear left at the Crooked Billet, re-joining the sea wall. Go under a road bridge then turn left along the road by the railway fence, with cockle sheds on the left. As the road bears left after ~¼ mile climb steps on the right to Leigh station.

The walk can be continued to Benfleet (11½ miles) by joining Walk 44.

Walk 44

LEIGH-ON-SEA – BENFLEET & CIRCULAR
4 / 7½ MILES

A well known Essex walk with excellent views, wildlife and historical interest. The circular walk can be started from Leigh (1), Benfleet (9) or Hadleigh (15). Frequent trains enable an easy return to the starting point for those walking in only one direction.

Start - Leigh-on-Sea station, Benfleet station or Hadleigh Farm

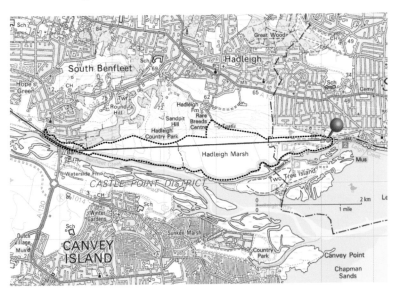

Parking: Leigh & Benfleet stations & towns (charged), Hadleigh
Train: Leigh & Benfleet (frequent)
Bus: Leigh & Benfleet (frequent)
Shops: Leigh & Benfleet (off route)

Refreshments: Pubs & cafés, Leigh & Benfleet (off route), bar/café at
Benfleet Moorings, café at Hadleigh Farm
Public Toilets: Benfleet & Leigh stations

1. Turn right out of station and immediately right over the railway
   bridge. When the road bends right after ~75 yards take a
   concrete path on the bank to the left.
2. On reaching a road by Leigh Motor Boat Club, to the right is a
   golf range with café and to the left the bridge to Two Tree Island,
   an interesting diversion to explore.

*The 640 acre Two Tree Island was reclaimed when a sea wall was built
around salt marsh, forming rough grazing land. Now a nature reserve,
its name comes from two large elms that were prominent until felled by
storms in 1965.*

3. Cross the road and continue on a hard track, with glimpses of
   Hadleigh Castle to the right. This is the Thames Estuary Path and
   continues on the winding sea wall opposite Two Tree Island, with
   a good view of the lagoon at its western end.
4. The path continues on the broad dyke (one of the widest in
   Essex) beside Benfleet Creek, with good views to the castle
   across Hadleigh Marsh.

*You are now walking through the 387 acre Hadleigh Country Park, one
of the largest and most varied in Essex, with a mix of woodland, pasture,
hay meadow and marsh. It is notable for large numbers of butterflies
and dragonflies. The park was venue for the London Olympics mountain
bike events and the track has now been adapted for public use.*

5. The path continues to Benfleet on the wide embankment.
   Canvey Island is over the water to the left and the cranes of
   London Gateway Docks can be seen in the distance.

*Much of the country park is owned by the Salvation Army, a legacy of
William Booth who purchased the land in 1890 and set up Home Farm
Colony where 'criminals, paupers, the reckless and helpless' received
training before being sent overseas. A line of posts in the creek are the
remains of General Booth's Jetty.*

6. As the path comes close to the railway line, go through a gate

where a sign advises 'BENFLEET MOORINGS – PRIVATE'. Access is permitted for walkers.

7. Follow the road running by the creek, passing a variety of boats moored on pontoons. Refreshments can be obtained from Barge Gladys, a vessel converted to a bar / café.

The creek, which was once much wider, was the site of a Saxon victory in the 9th century Battle of Benfleet. Invading Vikings under command of King Haesten were beaten by Saxon forces led by Edward, son of King Alfred. Charred timbers from Viking ships were found when the railway was constructed.

8. Pass Benfleet Flood Barrier, which was built in the 1970s to protect Canvey Island and Benfleet, then join Ferry Road by the bridge to Canvey. Continue along Ferry Road for ¼ mile to the railway station and bus stops.

9. If starting from Benfleet, or following the circular route, go under the bridge immediately outside the main station entrance. Turn right towards the car park, then left after 20 yards up Station Road.

10. On reaching School Lane (150 yards) turn right along a track, which splits after ⅔ mile. Both branches are signed for Hadleigh Castle but the right is preferred as this is 'pedestrian priority' so you will encounter fewer mountain bikes.

11. The well signed hard track descends towards the railway as it runs mainly between low trees. There are many grassy tracks which could be taken if preferred but this is the simplest and is all weather. If in doubt, follow 'pedestrian priority' signs, staying on the hard track closest to the railway.

12. After 2 miles (and ⅓ mile after the castle first comes into view) follow a footpath sign on the left beneath the castle. Follow the path then track up the hill. Looking back there are views to Canvey Island, Southend Pier and across the Thames to Kent.

13. The castle gate is reached after ¼ mile. Alternatively continue 250 yards up the track to Hadleigh Farm (Salvation Army) with café and rare breeds farm.

Strategically situated overlooking the Thames, Hadleigh Castle was built by Hubert de Burgh in 1215 and extensively refortified by Edward III during the Hundred Years War. It became a favourite residence of the ageing king who used to bring hunting parties here. Its unstable clay foundations and partial demolition (much of the stone was used for building churches) have left most of the castle a ruin, but two towers remain, one of which was used by Georgian revenue men looking out for smugglers.

14. After exploring the castle and enjoying the views, take a grassy path starting to the left of the main tower, which passes through two kissing gates and exits the castle grounds. Continue on the path along a descending ridge, turning left at a double kissing gate at the bottom.

15. The path runs alongside a field, straight on at another gate after 200 yards, then after ½ mile through a gateway to a paved roadway. Follow this for 200 yards to the main road, then turn right reaching Leigh station after 250 yards.

16. If returning to Benfleet follow directions from 1. A diversion into the picturesque Old Leigh village with its pubs and cafés can be made by taking a path to the left immediately after crossing the railway bridge.

The walk can be extended to Pitsea or around Bowers Marsh by continuing at 8 onto Walk 46.

Walk 45

CANVEY ISLAND CIRCULAR
6½ / 8½ / 15 MILES

*A varied walk on the sea walls of Canvey Island, alongside creeks and
the River Thames and passing one of our more unlikely nature reserves.
Contrary to Canvey's reputation, there is no oil refinery and storage tanks
cover just a small proportion of the island. The walk can be split into 6½
and 8½ mile sections by using the bus to Concord Beach.*

Start - Benfleet station or Concord Beach.

Parking: Benfleet station, Concord Beach
Train: Benfleet (frequent)
Bus: Benfleet, Canvey (regular)
Shops: Benfleet, Canvey

Refreshments: Several cafes & pubs along the route.
Public Toilets: Benfleet station, Smallgains Marina, Concord Beach

England's 6th largest island, Canvey was largely agricultural until the 20th century but its character changed as the population grew and large oil and gas terminals were constructed. Much of its land is reclaimed and below sea level, the first walls having been built by 14th century Dutch engineers, many of whom stayed on and were given land for their work. Sea defences were overwhelmed in the Great Flood of 1953 and 58 lives lost.

If starting from Concord Beach follow instructions from 8. Without the diversion to Benfleet station the walk is ½ mile shorter.

1. Turn left from the main exit of Benfleet station, following the road for ¼ mile to Canvey Bridge. Prior to construction of the first bridge here in 1931, access to Canvey was by ferry or low tide stepping stones.

2. 100 yards beyond the bridge take a footpath on the left, which crosses a roadway after 200 yards, then leads onto the concrete sea wall (some way back from the creek). Turn left onto the wall which is followed for the 14½ mile circuit of the island.

3. Castle Point Golf Club is on your right and to the left views soon open up to Hadleigh Castle, then Southend and its pier. The sea wall bends right after 1½ miles, then left after a further 600 yards, running above a road.

4. Stay on the sea wall when the houses end after 1 mile and as it bends right opposite Smallgains Marina, then head up Smallings

Creek. At the head of the creek turn left along an embankment, with a small lake and football pitches to your right, then soon turn left again onto the right bank of the creek.

5. Cross the entrance road to the marina (there are toilets and a café just inside) and stay on the sea wall as it soon bends right opposite Island Yacht Club. A two mile detour may be made by following a path from here across salt marsh to Canvey Point, but note that parts of this flood at high tide.

6. The Thames is reached after ¼ mile, where the wall turns sharp right. Now heading west you may proceed either at the top of the wall or on a paved path below it that runs above the beach.

7. Concord Beach (with sand!) is reached after 1 mile. Here are two paddling pools (saved from closure by the local council) and some excellent murals depicting Canvey's history. After a further ¼ mile The Labworth Café is reached.

This 1930s concrete building was designed to resemble the bridge of the Queen Mary. After a period of neglect and narrowly escaping demolition, the top floor was reopened as a restaurant in the late 1990s, with a beach bistro added later on the ground floor.

8. Turn inland here for shops, cafes, toilets and pubs, and for the bus back to Benfleet. (Buses run from Furtherwick Road just inland of a small park).

9. At Canvey Bay, another sandy beach, the path continues inland of the sea wall, soon passing Scar House Pumping Station, one of thirteen which help prevent Canvey flooding.

10. The island's oil storage depots are soon reached, occupying just a mile of coastline. The path dives under pipelines to two of the several jetties along this stretch.

11. After passing The Lobster Smack, a weatherboard inn dating from the 17th century, the sea wall bends right heading up Holehaven Creek. The long jetty extending into the Thames was built by Occidental to serve a new oil refinery which was never built.

12. The next six miles are rural walking, initially opposite the closed Coryton Refinery, beyond which the embankment is grass topped.

To the right is Canvey Wick, a nature reserve with as many species per square metre as a rainforest and one of the most important UK sites for endangered invertebrates. Earmarked for an oil refinery and covered with thousands of tonnes of silt from the Thames, nature took over when the site was abandoned after the discovery of North Sea Oil led to cancellation of the development.

13. Just beyond a ruined wooden dock the path turns right by Creek Flood Barrier, now following East Haven Creek for 2 miles until passing under the A130 viaduct. Veering right the embankment takes you along Benfleet Creek then inland of an area of salt marsh.

14. On reaching a road turn left across the bridge for Benfleet station, or if continuing around the island, cross the road and rejoin the embankment.

WALK 46

BENFLEET – PITSEA OR BENFLEET CIRCULAR
4 MILES (4½ / 6½ MILES CIRCULAR)

A circular walk starting along Benfleet Creek, passing through an RSPB reserve with a longer option to explore the reserve, and returning to Benfleet, or continuing to Pitsea from where frequent trains allow an easy return to the starting point. Note that the longer route passes through an RSPB reserve where dogs are not permitted.

Start – Benfleet station / Finish – Pitsea station

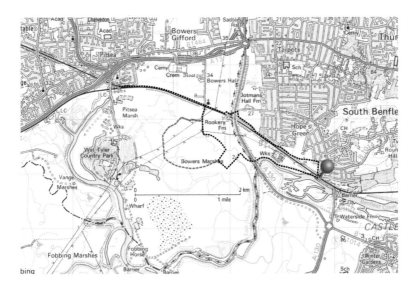

Parking: Benfleet & Pitsea stations & towns, RSPB Bowers Marsh
Train: Benfleet, Pitsea (frequent)
Bus: Benfleet, Pitsea (frequent)
Shops: Benfleet, Pitsea (off route)

Refreshments: Pubs & cafés, Benfleet, Pitsea (off route). Kiosks at stations
Public Toilets: Benfleet & Pitsea stations

1. Turn left out of the main station entrance, cross the road by bus stops and turn right along a path running on the low embankment beside Benfleet Creek. Immediately before the railway bridge turn left onto a path.

2. Stay on the path as it bears away from the creek by houseboats and runs between hedges, then alongside a metal security fence. The path here is little used and can get a bit overgrown.

3. On meeting another fence, pass though the gap and continue by the original fence, coming out in a field with a sewage works at the far end.

4. Keep to the left of the field and turn left in the corner where a signpost shows the Thames Estuary Path. If the path is unclear head for a point 3 yards from the corner of a barbed-wire-topped fence, then towards a metal spiked fence.

5. Go through the gap at the end of the fence. The path continues parallel to the creek, then drops down to the water's edge after 150 yards. It can however be overgrown in which case an alternative is along a rarely used motocross track until turning left down to the creek.

6. Pass under the A130 bridge and climb a few steps on the right. The expanse of marshland ahead is Bowers Marsh RSPB Reserve and in summer the field can be a mass of wild flowers.

After careful restoration of ancient grazing marsh, creating 260 hectares of wetland habitat, the RSPB opened its Bowers Marsh reserve in 2013. Hard paths allow access to the saline and freshwater lagoons, scrapes, ditches, reedbeds and areas of wet grassland, which support waders and wildfowl. A lucky visitor might spot a water vole.

7. A Thames Estuary Path sign points across the field but paths actually run further left or around the edge. The latter is easier to find. Turn right, following the path around the field.

8. On reaching a gravel track turn right, following RSPB signs to car park, branching left though a gate after 300 yards and left again at a barn. Alternatively, for the longer route around the reserve, continue straight on following the gravel path signposted Great Pound. The winding path passes lagoons rich in birdlife, eventually meeting the reserve access road.

9. Turn right at the car park along the path parallel with the road, then left onto the access road, passing under the railway and coming out by St Margaret's Church. If continuing to Pitsea follow instructions from A. If returning to Benfleet walk through the churchyard and continue from 10.

St Margaret's Church dates from the 14th century but there has been a church on this site since Saxon times. Its isolated position is probably explained by the church having been built between the two manors of Bowers; Earls Fee and Bowers Hall. During the 18th century it was used as a barn and in 1829 much rebuilding was required when the vaults collapsed as a result of graves having been dug too close to the foundations. More recently repairs were required after woodpeckers made forty holes in the steeple.

10. Leave the churchyard through a gap in the hedge in the right hand corner and follow a path by the railway. Turn left on reaching a lane by another bridge.

11. 70 yards after passing under the A130 cross a stile on the right and follow the right edge of the field, crossing four more stiles.

12. A fifth stile at the end of the field takes you to a path which soon meets a road before continuing between back gardens and the railway.

13. On emerging onto playing fields turn right onto a tarmac path. After ⅓ mile turn left over a footbridge then immediately right onto an embankment. This is followed back to the railway bridge by Benfleet station, turning right at a T junction and passing two stone sculptures depicting the Battle of Benfleet. Pass under the bridge and return to the station.

A. Follow the path on the left immediately after the railway bridge, running beside the railway towards Pitsea. This passes alongside a field, then after crossing a footbridge, along the edge of scrubland.

B. Pass through a gate in the corner, entering a dark passageway between the railway fence and back gardens. If preferred, go through the first gap and continue along Brackendale Avenue.

C. Turn left on reaching a T junction and cross the bridge over the railway. Pitsea station is immediately on the left.

Pitsea, once a small village, but now swallowed up by Basildon, doesn't have the best of reputations. Its centre consists mainly of 1970s concrete and the first Tesco Extra to open in Britain. Its one building of historical interest, the 13th century (but much rebuilt) Church of St Michael, fell into ruin and just the tower remains as a landmark on the hill.

It's possible to continue to Stanford-le-Hope or East Tilbury following the Thames Estuary Path from opposite Pitsea station, crossing Fobbing Marshes & linking with Walk 47 at 4.

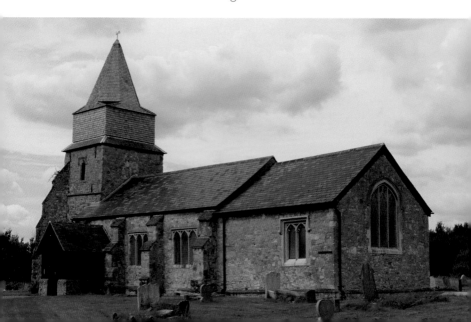

WALK 47

STANFORD-LE-HOPE – EAST TILBURY OR THAMESIDE NATURE PARK CIRCULAR
7 / 5 MILES

An easy walk with good views of the Thames, passing through Thurrock Thameside Nature Park, which is taking over the former Mucking landfill tip. This area has seen more changes in recent years than any other on the Essex coast and will continue to alter as the nature park expands

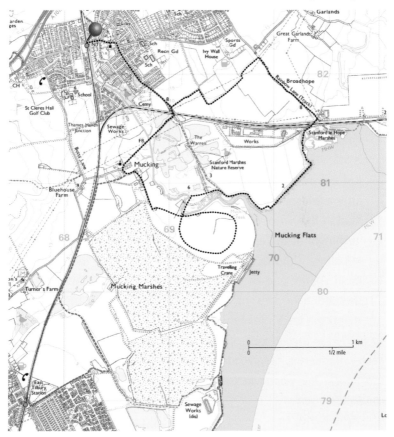

over the remainder of the landfill site. Paths may therefore change but will be signed. Options are a 5 mile circular route starting at Thameside Nature Park, or Stanford-le-Hope, or to continue to East Tilbury.

Start - Stanford-le-Hope station / Finish – East Tilbury station
Or circular from Thurrock Thameside Nature Park

Parking: Stanford-le-Hope, East Tilbury, Thameside Nature Park
Train: Stanford-le-Hope, East Tilbury (both regular)
Bus: Stanford-le-Hope (regular), East Tilbury (limited)
Shops: Stanford-le-Hope, East Tilbury
Refreshments: Stanford-le-Hope, East Tilbury, Thameside Nature Park
Public Toilets: Thameside Nature Park

The 5 mile circular walk can be started from Stanford-le-Hope station (extra mile), or by parking in Wharf Road (1), or at Thurrock Thameside Nature Park (7). The walk can be shortened by using Wharf Road to more directly enter or exit the Nature Park. Note that some of the paths in the nature park are not yet shown on Ordnance Survey maps.

1. Turn right from Stanford-le-Hope station, pass St Margaret's Church then after 350 yards turn right down Wharf Road, which is followed for ½ mile.

2. Just before a railway bridge take a paved track on the left, then after a few yards Footpath 38 which runs along the left edge of a field to the left of pylons.

3. Turn right at the end of the field, passing under the pylons, then left after 175 yards into the next field, walking to the right of the ditch. At the end of this field walk through a tunnel of bushes then continue straight on along the left edge of the field until meeting a track (Rainbow Lane).

To the left is a good view of the huge London Gateway Port. With six deep-water berths, twenty-four giant cranes and a new rail link, the port can handle the world's largest container ships and up to 3.5 million containers a year.

4. When the track ends after ½ mile by an electricity sub-

station continue on the footpath over a crossing of the port railway, emerging onto the river wall. Turn right along the high embankment walking beside a bay.

5. On meeting a gravel track after ¾ mile continue straight on along the grassy embankment. Turn left at a gate after 250 yards, then right after 125 yards, heading up Mucking Creek.

6. After 250 yards pass through a gate on the sluice at the head of the creek, entering Thurrock Thameside Nature Park. Continue straight on at a double gate after 100 yards, walking on the right side of the creek and reaching the Visitor Centre after ½ mile.

The former Mucking landfill site is being transformed by Essex Wildlife Trust into a living landscape with habitat for coastal and wetland wildlife. Opened in 2013 by Sir David Attenborough, the 120 acres of nature park will eventually expand to 845 acres with 12 miles of footpaths. It is already hosting populations of barn owls, water voles, harvest mice, skylarks, butterflies and invertebrates. The innovative visitor centre gives superb views of the park and the Thames.

7. From the Visitor Centre follow a path on the left of the car park, initially running parallel with the road. To the left are cranes which transferred London's waste from barges. After ~½ mile the path crosses the access road, soon reaching the path above Mucking Creek.

8. Turn left at the gate then left again at the double gate above the sluice that you passed through on the outward route from Stanford. Head away from the creek, following a path that meets the access road again after ¼ mile.

9. For East Tilbury follow instructions from A. For the circular route continue on the road out of the Nature Park, passing a white farmhouse that was formerly the Crown Inn.

The tiny village of Mucking is one of the most historically important in Essex, with prehistoric, Roman and Saxon settlements here. There was said to be a smugglers' tunnel linking the Crown Inn to Mucking Creek, where Thames barges berthed with cargoes both legal and illicit.

10. 250 yards from the park exit, in the corner just before the churchyard (privately owned), turn right onto a footpath which

crosses Stanford Warren Nature Reserve. The path passes between reed beds, some of the largest in Essex, then alongside Warren Lakes.

11. Stay on the path as it bends right after ½ mile, running above then joining a lane. Turn left onto the lane, passing under the railway bridge.

12. To return to Stanford-le-Hope continue along Wharf Road, following the outward route. For Thameside Nature Park turn right 125 yards after the railway bridge, following Footpath 68 and instructions from 2.

A. After 125 yards turn left onto a track just beyond farm buildings. This crosses a roadway after ¼ mile then bends left, running alongside the railway.

B. Bear left at the end of a large lake (~1 mile) passing between the lake and a pond, then after ¼ mile follow the path as it bends right. Turn right at a gate after 0.4 miles and follow the path into East Tilbury (stay to the left of the park). On reaching the road the station is 70 yards on the right

To link with Walk 48 towards Coalhouse Fort, turn right at the gate at B.

WALK 48

EAST TILBURY - TILBURY
7½ MILES

A walk along the banks of the Thames passing two historic forts. The whole walk can be followed as a linear route with return by train, or out and back along the Two Forts Way (also 7½ miles total), parking at Coalhouse Fort and walking along the river to Tilbury Fort or the Worlds End.

Start – East Tilbury station or Coalhouse Fort / Finish – Tilbury Town station

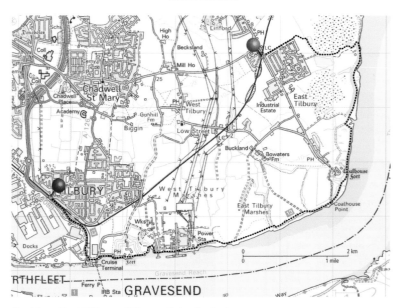

Parking: East Tilbury, Tilbury & both forts
Train: East Tilbury, Tilbury (regular)
Bus: East Tilbury, Tilbury Fort, Tilbury (limited)

Shops: East Tilbury, Tilbury (off route)
Refreshments: Pubs & cafés, East Tilbury (off route), Tilbury (World's End)
Public Toilets: None on route

Tilbury Fort is owned by English Heritage and open most days, however Coalhouse Fort opens only a few days each year.

1. Turn right from East Tilbury station, cross the road and take a footpath on the left after 60 yards. The path runs alongside Gobions Park. Pass through a gate after ¼ mile, ignore a branch to the right and stay on the path as it bends right.

2. On reaching a junction don't go through the gate (this leads to Thameside Nature Park) but take the path on the right which runs between bushes, reaching the river wall after almost a mile. Here are good views back to London Gateway Docks and across the water to Kent marshes.

3. Turn right, walking along a concrete path on the river side of the wall. After a mile leave the concrete wall, taking a path on the left running below an earth embankment close to the shore. Pass through a gate and continue left of the wide moat of Coalhouse Fort.

Constructed between 1861 and 1874, Coalhouse Fort was built to defend the Thames from potential invasion by France. Forts were also built on the opposite side of the Thames in Kent, at Cliffe and Shorenmead. It served as a coastal defence battery during WW1 and WW2 and a Degaussing Monitor Station to help protect shipping from magnetic mines deployed in the Thames estuary. After years of neglect the fort was leased from Thurrock Council in 1983 and is being gradually refurbished.

4. To enter the fort or car park follow a path on the right which runs in front of, then round the second lake. A further option is to return to East Tilbury station along the road (1½ miles) or use the infrequent bus service. For Tilbury continue straight on, soon reaching a strange hexagonal tower by the river.

Marked on maps for many years as a water tower, this was in fact a disguise for its use as an early WW2 radar tower, positioned like the fort at this strategic point where the Thames narrows. (It was once the first point inland where cannons positioned on both banks could cover the full width of the river).

5. Continue on a paved path to the right of the river wall. On the beaches glass and ceramics from a long abandoned land fill site can be seen and some interesting finds may be made.

6. Approaching the now closed Tilbury Power Station the path drops down to the water's edge on the river side of a concrete wall. Cranes and hoppers to the left were for the huge quantity of coal used by the power station.

7. The path runs under the jetty (note this can flood for a short while on the highest tides) and continues alongside the Thames. At the tip of a small creek steps lead up to the river wall. Take these and turn left, soon reaching Tilbury Fort.

Construction of Tilbury Fort was started by Charles II in 1672, following a disastrous attack by the Dutch on the English fleet in the Medway. Now under the care of English Heritage, it is one of the best preserved bastioned fortifications in Britain and other than some 19th century modifications, is in largely the same condition now as it was in the late 17th century. The fort's sole military success was in the First World War, when anti-aircraft guns on the parade ground shot down a Zeppelin airship.

8. Pass the Worlds End, a famous Essex pub (there has been a watering hole on this site since the 17th century and Samuel Pepys mentions visiting it in his diary), and stay by the river for a short distance until reaching two large buildings.

The first of these was Tilbury Riverside station, which closed in 1992 and holds an important place in our history. It was at these docks that the Empire Windrush bought the first immigrants from the West Indies in 1948. For many thousands of Commonwealth citizens a train ride from here to London was their introduction to Britain. The second is London Cruise Terminal, London's only purpose-built deep water cruise facility.

9. The final mile of the walk is along roads, although if preferred a bus runs to Tilbury Town station. Turn right at the roundabout after the cruise terminal then straight on at the next roundabout.

10. A path runs between the road and docks, becoming a pavement after a while. For the town cross a footbridge over the railway and for Tilbury Town station continue along the road.

There is no public access to the Thames at Tilbury Docks, so it's necessary to use roads to reach Grays and link with Walk 49.

WALK 49

GRAYS - PURFLEET
5 MILES

An interesting, if not traditionally scenic walk along the industrial Thames, including a little used path passing under the Queen Elizabeth Bridge. The working, derelict and redeveloped wharves, jetties and industry make this quite different to all the other Essex walks. Regular trains allow an easy return to Grays.

Start – Grays station / Finish – Purfleet station

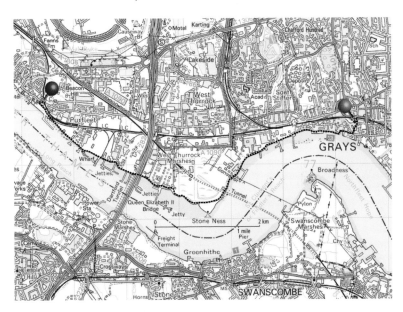

Parking: Grays town, Purfleet station & road
Train: Grays, Purfleet (regular)
Bus: Grays, Purfleet (regular)

Shops: Grays, Purfleet
Refreshments: Pubs & cafés, Grays, pub Purfleet (off route),
Public Toilets: Grays station & town

1. Turn right out of Grays station then immediately right across a
    level crossing, continuing downhill with the River Thames ahead.
    Cross the road and walk under the sign 'Grays Town Wharf'.

*Once a hive of activity, with coal, oil and timber being brought ashore,
factories, barge builders and ship breakers, Grays waterfront has been
largely replaced rather than restored. New houses and apartments now
line the river.*

2. Head right around the wharf and continue as the path turns right,
    taking you beside the river, around several old docks and past The
    Wharf pub.

*One of the few old buildings remaining on the waterfront, The Wharf is
the last place for refreshment before the walk ends. Its modern clientele
is somewhat different from the seafarers and wharfmen who once drank
here.*

3. On reaching a metal fence, climb steps over the sea wall to Grays
    Terminal Number Two Jetty. Here the character of the walk
    changes instantly as you pass factories and wharves, some still
    working and others long abandoned.

4. Follow a narrow path to the right which runs by the water for the next two miles, with occasional short tunnels under jetties.

About a mile of river wall is covered with street art, the varied designs and bright colours making an unusual accompaniment to a coastal walk. Whilst not strictly legal, the art is tolerated and painters can sometimes be seen here working on their individual sections.

5. The path bears right by a triangle of salt marsh at Stone Ness, where a small lighthouse has been warning ships of the headland since 1885. From here a fine view opens up of the Queen Elizabeth II Bridge.

6. Take a slope over the river wall and continue on the path inside the wall, passing Vopak oil terminal and Lafarge cement works, before reaching the QE2 Bridge.

Walking beneath what was once Europe's longest cable-supported bridge provides a view and a sense of the structure's size that few see. With towers that rise 190 metres, the bridge contains 145,000 cubic metres of concrete and 1,500 tonnes of galvanised steel.

7. After a short section by the water a zig zag slope takes the path back over the river wall and along what might be the least scenic stretch of coast path in Britain. There is no view of the water, but to the right is the huge Cobelfreight terminal.

8. On reaching a derelict site (Thames Board Mills paper mill once stood here) follow footpath signs away from the river. These direct walkers through the site running parallel with the railway. Note that this area is due for development in which case the path route may be changed but it should still be signed.

9. The path bends right ~100 yards before the Cornwall Oil Terminal, passes through a gate and emerges opposite Purfleet station.

The walk can be extended to Rainham (10½ miles) or a loop around Rainham Marshes by joining the start of Walk 50.

Walk 50

PURFLEET - RAINHAM & PURFLEET CIRCULAR
BOTH ROUTES 5½ MILES

A walk on hard paths along the banks of the Thames and across Rainham Marshes, passing a major RSPB nature reserve and sites of historical interest. The circular walk starts from RSPB Visitor Centre (3).

Start – Purfleet station or RSPB Rainham Marshes / Finish – Rainham station

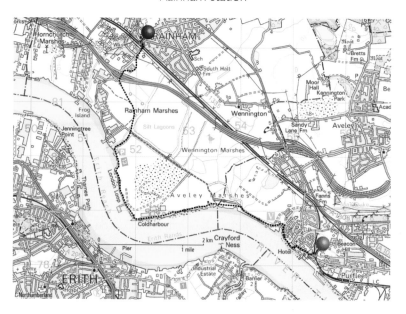

Parking: Purfleet & Rainham stations, RSPB, Aveley Bay, Coldharbour
Train: Purfleet, Rainham (regular)
Bus: Purfleet, Rainham (regular)

Shops: Purfleet, Rainham (off route)
Refreshments: Pubs Purfleet, café RSPB, Pubs & cafés Rainham (off route)
Public Toilets: RSPB Visitor Centre

1. Turn right from Purfleet station, passing Cornwall Oil Terminal and Botany Terrace Cottages. Cross the road just before a roundabout and turn left opposite St Stephen's Church, along a path signed 'Thames Path'.
2. Follow the path along the river wall, passing in front of the Royal Hotel.

On your right you pass the last remaining of five buildings which housed the Royal Gunpowder Magazines that moved here from Greenwich in 1760, when it was considered too dangerous to store explosive so close to London. Each building could hold 10,400 barrels of gunpowder, with the site guarded by a garrison of soldiers. The building is open to the public as Purfleet Heritage Centre.

3. Cross a footbridge over the Mar Dyke to reach the RSPB Visitor Centre.

450,000 years ago the Mar Dyke and River Darent opposite in Kent were a single river but were cut in half when Ice Age glaciers forced the Thames southwards. A metal sculpture by the bridge depicts a wedding ring and contains list of significant dates in Purfleet's history. A military railway once ran inland from the Mar Dyke jetty.

4. Continue on the sea wall with views across the reserve to the
    HS1 high speed railway and A13 viaduct. If the tide is low a Saxon
    sea wall can be seen in the river.

*After more than a hundred years of military use the RSPB bought the
marshes in 2000 and transformed them into an important area for
nature with easy access for the public. Fifteen miles of ditches were
unblocked, facilitating movement of water, with sluices constructed to
allow the water level adjustment to maximise available habitat. A wide
variety of birds can be seen, with large numbers of sea-breeding waders
in summer and huge flocks of ducks and geese in winter. There is an easy
two mile walk around the reserve on hard paths and boardwalks.*

5. Take the left fork, staying on the embankment where a tarmac
    path leaves to the right and follow the path around Aveley Bay.
    At low tide the mudflats here attract many birds and some rare
    species have been spotted.

6. Just before a metal gate take a narrow path on the left which joins
    a tarmac path after a few yards. There is a small car park here. A
    post indicates that it is 6km to Rainham station and further posts
    every 200 metres keep walkers informed of their progress.

7. The path takes you around a landfill site, past a disused wharf, then
    some industrial units, before bending right by a red beacon at
    Coldharbour Point, one of nine navigational lights on the Thames.
    There has been a landfill operation on this site since 1906. Steam

locomotives once ran from the riverside hauling railway wagons filled with waste to dropping points around the site.

8. Stay on the river wall path, which soon reaches a refuse handling station where barges still bring London's rubbish to be buried.

Coldharbour was once an island separated from the mainland by tidal creeks. A ferry ran from here to Erith across the river. It was known as the 'short ferry' as opposed to the 'long ferry' which called at Rainham on the route from Gravesend to London.

9. Ford's Dagenham car plant can now be seen just beyond a bend in the river. The path continues on the river wall, reaching a small bay where 16 'concrete barges' lie on the mud.

The concrete barges weren't for carrying concrete; they were actually made of it, reinforced with steel. A number were built during WW2 and the vessels lying abandoned on the Thames mud are the largest concentration remaining. Their exact use is unclear. Some sources say they were involved in the D Day landings, carrying fuel or as part of the Mulberry Harbours, but others suggest that they were simply barges made from concrete due to the wartime shortage of steel.

10. Turn away from the river by the barges, walking through a car park and following the road inland.

11. Coldharbour Lane is reached after 0.4 miles. If returning to Purfleet turn right and continue from 13. For Rainham follow instructions from A.

12. Follow the footpath which runs to the right of Coldharbour Lane, then crosses the road after 0.7 miles and heads across Wennington Marshes. Raised pipes running across and alongside the road once carried silt dredged from the Thames to silt lagoons on the marshes.

13. After ~1 mile the path rejoins the Thames embankment, which is followed back to the RSPB visitor centre.

A. Turn left over a bridge, left onto the road, then after 50 yards right over a footbridge to a path across the marshes.

B. Follow the path as it crosses Rainham Marshes until reaching a roundabout by the A13. Cross the slip road at a pedestrian crossing, walk under the viaduct, then cross the next slip road, again at a pedestrian crossing. Turn right over a footbridge onto another path across marshes which takes you almost to the station.

C. Where the path forks, take the right-hand option leading to a long bridge over the HS1 railway line and down to a level crossing over the London, Tilbury & Southend line. The crossing is unusual in that the road only runs for a few yards, having been severed by the high speed line. Proceed over the crossing to the station or town.

ALSO BY PETER CATON

ESSEX COAST WALK

When Peter Caton set out to walk the Essex coast he had no idea of the beauty, wildlife and stories that he would find on the way. He takes the reader up and down the many creeks and estuaries of the longest coastline of any English county, through nature reserves, seaside resorts, unspoilt villages, sailing centres and alongside industry past and present. On the way we read of tales of witchcraft, ghosts, smuggling, bigamy and incest. We learn of the county's varied history – stories of battles with Vikings, of invading Romans bringing elephants, a fort where the only casualty occurred in a cricket match, burning Zeppelins and of Jack the Ripper.

Whilst an entertaining narrative, not a guidebook, Essex Coast Walk contains a wealth of information, including many littleknown facts and stories. With gentle humour to match the coastline's gentle beauty, and illustrated with photographs and maps, the book makes for easy reading.

The book highlights how climate change may alter our coast and looks at new methods of coping with rising sea levels. It tells us how tiny settlements grew into large holiday resorts and how other villages have remained as unspoilt and isolated communities. The author's thought provoking final reflections consider how the coast has changed over the centuries and what its future may be.

Written in an accessible style, Essex Coast Walk has been enjoyed not only by those living in the county, but by others who have been surprised to read of the beauty and history of this little known part of our coast.

£9.99 376 PAGES ISBN 9781848761162 **Published by Matador, reprinted & updated 2016**

ALSO BY PETER CATON

SUFFOLK COAST WALK

Combining travel writing with a walking guide,
Suffolk Coast Walk provides a wonderful insight into this fascinating county
and is the companion book to Essex Coast Walk by the same author.

Peter Caton explores all 162 miles of Suffolk's unique coastline, describing the route for fellow walkers, with an engaging narrative that tells of the beauty, history and wildlife of this mysterious and varied coast.

The reader is taken up and down Suffolk's remote creeks and rivers, past sandy beaches and huge expanses of shingle, through nature reserves, seaside resorts and tiny villages. We learn of the county's abundant wildlife, not just through its famous bird populations but also of equally interesting and less celebrated creatures, and how habitats are managed to balance the needs of nature and mankind.

Throughout his journey, Peter uncovers many mysteries and considers the stories behind legends of Anne Boleyn, invading Germans, a halfman half-fish character, UFOs, Crazy Mary and bells tolling beneath the sea. He visits Suffolk's only island and takes a boat trip to investigate the secret world of Orford Ness.

More than 100 colour and black & white photos illustrate the story of the walk and the beauty and atmosphere of county's remarkable coast. With maps at the start of each chapter, this is a book for those who enjoy a short stroll, a longer ramble or simply wish to follow the coast from the comfort of an armchair.

£9.99 272pp ISBN 9781784620967 **Published by Matador**

ALSO BY PETER CATON

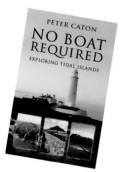

NO BOAT REQUIRED
EXPLORING TIDAL ISLANDS

When is an island not an island?
Peter Caton takes us to all four corners of England, Scotland and Wales
to find out.

Sharing our nation's fascination with islands, Peter sets out to be the first person to visit all 43 tidal islands which can be walked to from the UK mainland. Along the way he faces many challenges: precipitous cliffs, vicious dogs, disappearing footpaths, lost bus drivers, fast tides, quicksand and enormous quantities of mud, but also experiences wonderfully scenic journeys by road, rail and on foot. He contrasts the friendly welcome from most islanders and owners with the reluctance of others to permit visits, and tells how he was thrown off one secret island.

An entertaining narrative illustrated with colour photographs, No Boat Required contains a wealth of information as the author unearths many little known facts and stories. It tells of the solitude of the many remote islands and the difficulties of balancing the needs of people and wildlife. We learn of the islands' varied histories – stories of pirates, smugglers, murder and ghosts, of battles with Vikings, an island claimed by punks and another with its own king. He writes of the beauty of the islands and our coast, and reflects on how these may be affected by climate change.

In No Boat Required Peter Caton takes us to explore islands, some familiar but most which few of us know exist and even fewer have visited. He finds that our tidal islands are special places, many with fascinating and amusing stories and each one of them different. It adds up to a unique journey around Britain.

£12.99 344pp ISBN 9781848767010 **Published by Matador**

ALSO BY PETER CATON

THE NEXT STATION STOP

*A 10,000 mile tour of Britain, discovering what
it's like to travel on our modern railways and comparing experiences with
train journeys made over the last fifty years.*

Inspired by finding a childhood notebook, the author revisits locations
of family holidays, looking at how the journeys and places have changed,
and wondering why his parents chose such unlikely destinations.

His travels take him to some of the most beautiful and remote parts
of the country and on trains so eccentric that sometimes he wonders
if Thomas the Tank Engine is round the corner. Sampling a selection
of Inter City routes, he questions whether the pursuit of speed and
efficiency has taken away some of the enjoyment of travelling by train,
but on sleepers to Cornwall and Scotland finds the romance of rail
travel is still alive. He ends with a journey to Italy, with a diversion
up a snowy mountain, comparing European train travel with British
railways.

We read of the author's experiences of missed connections, inflexible
computers, waving to Marjory and upsetting a machine gun carrying
policeman. He writes of his frustrations with 'health & safety' and
ridiculous announcements, and how these combine to give the book
its title.

Illustrated with sixty colour photographs covering the steam, diesel
and electric eras of the last 50 years, The Next Station Stop will
appeal to anyone who travels on Britain's trains.

£9.99 260pp ISBN 978-1-78306-050-4 **Published by Matador**

ALSO BY PETER CATON

STAND UP SIT DOWN
A CHOICE TO WATCH
FOOTBALL

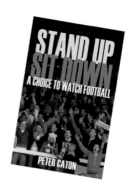

For a hundred years most supporters watched football from terraces, a culture that was an integral part of the game. By the 1980s though, neglected stadia, hooliganism and a lack of concern for safety meant that football had to change, and after 96 Liverpool fans tragically died at Hillsborough, Lord Taylor's report recommended that our grounds should be all-seated. Many people however believe that something of the soul has been taken away from watching football and that standing is the natural way to feel part of the game.

In Stand Up Sit Down Peter Caton considers the arguments for and against the choice to stand to watch football. He visits the 23 English grounds that still have terraces, seeking the views of clubs and supporters, travels to Yorkshire to watch rugby league and to Germany to stand on a convertible terrace.

With extensively researched background, the author analyses the disasters and hooliganism that led to all-seating, and the many changes that have occurred in the game. He considers various solutions proposed to allow standing, and highlights obstacles facing those backing the choice to stand. His own experiences of watching football at all levels add insight and interest. The book ends by asking its own questions and with a whiff of conspiracy.

Illustrated with colour photographs, Stand Up Sit Down is a fascinating read, which unearths some surprising facts and raises many controversial issues relevant to all who love football.

£9.99 320pp ISBN 9781780881775 **Published by Matador**